The Dav

Anecdotes and Stories
from
Inside & Outside The Box

By
Carl Davenport

Printed by
High Quality Printing, Cork
Tel: +353 (0) 21 4353000

**Front Cover Image courtesy of the late MICHAEL OLNEY
of The Cork Examiner**

ACKNOWLEDGEMENTS:

I HAVE written this book based on my memories of the football and social scene in Cork in those heady days of the late 1960's and early 70's.

It has been written in my own hand without the use of a ghost-writer, written as I speak and you will note the absence of long, fancy words and maybe the grammar is not all it should be, but it must be appreciated that I was only a secondary schoolboy who progressed into football at a young age and was then educated in the school of life, which to my mind has perhaps been better than a university degree!

I have mentioned situations and occurrences that I have not previously discussed or brought up and hopefully I will raise a smile or two.

I have mentioned situations in these pages that may surprise a few, but hopefully will not shock you, the reader.

I have delved into the past and those great memories and those great days of soccer, show bands, Christy Ring and 'Pecker' Dunne and 'when we were young' on Leeside.

I have really enjoyed delving into the depths of my past and my ageing mind and equally enjoyed re-living those memories and I sincerely hope that you will also gain some pleasure and amusement in reading this book.

It would be remiss of me not to mention and thank profusely some of the people who have worked the oracle in getting this book into the light of day.

And by way of acknowledgement, I must first of all say a big 'Thank You' to Ann and Jim Casey of Express Secretarial, Cork for all their help and patience in typing the entire book from my own hand written scrawl (sorry notes), to the 96FM crew - Neil Prenderville, Barry O'Mahony and Trevor Welch, to my friends in the Cork media - Noel Spillane, Billy George and John Roycroft for all their expertise, help and assistance in bringing four long years of endeavour and writer's cramp to fruition.

To my dear friend, Alice De la Cour in the Irish Examiner for her advice and encouragement and to Anthony Dinan, Diarmuid O'Donovan and Brian Lougheed for their valued input.

A big thanks to Vivien Duggan of the Ambassador Hotel, Military Hill for her inspiration and aupport.

To Plunkett Carter, a football historian if ever there was one who lives opposite 'the Box' and to football lovers and fanatics like myself - Gerry Desmond, Patsy Dorgan, John Lawson, Noel O'Mahony, Ray Cowhie and Frank Connolly who all agreed to be interviewed and contributed in no small way to the publication of my memoirs.

To my dear friend and Kerry GAA legend Mick O'Connell from Valentia Island and not forgetting life-long friends and mates of mine in and around Bolton like big Sam Allardyce, Francis Lee and the late Alan Ball who won a World Cup winners medal with England at Wembley in 1966.

To the Kinsale crew of Jim Good and Jimmy Edwards and to great sportsmen like Billy Morgan, Jimmy Barry Murphy, Denis Coughlan, John Carroll, Donie Leahy, Jackie Morley, Pat O'Mahony, Alfie Hale, John Keogh, Al Finucane and Kevin Fitzpatrick, Noel Murphy, Eric Philpott, Tommy O'Leary and Jerry Finnegan, Ollan Kelleher, Pat Dineen, Barry McGann - a warm and sincere 'Thank You' to you all.

CARL.

FOREWORD BY SAM ALLARDYCE

I have known Carl, commonly known as "The Dav" for the best part of 30 years.

I never realised just how popular he was in southern Ireland until he asked me to take my then team Bolton Wanderers Football Club to play a Testimonial for him against his former club.

We got well looked after as always, and I was amazed on the night that we got a complete sell-out for his game.

In our early days, he talked about what a good footballer he was and he liked flashing his medal on the big gold chain he wore around his neck.

I called him "Medallion Man" not realising it was his pride and joy, as it was the medal he won playing for Cork, when he represented them in Europe.

He still thinks he is management material and will ring me after a game and say - "We were good today" if we won or if we lost "you will have to do something with that back four."

I sincerely hope the book is a great success.

I know 'the Dav' has put a lot of hard work, time and effort into it over the last four years or so, and if he writes as good as he tells stories, I am in no doubt it will be.

Sam Allardyce.

FRANNIE LEE ON 'THE DAV'

WHAT can I say?

He's most likely told you all there is to know.

I have known Carl for over 50 years and we joined Bolton Wanderers together on the same day back in 1957.

Before that we played in the Bolton Boys Federation against one other. I played with a team called Winrows and Carl was with Farnworth Boys Club. He will tell you that they always beat us, and they did, and who always got the goals, yes he did.

We had some happy times together at Bolton Wanderers and we'd always play snooker together after training at a temperance bar, just across the road from the old Burnden Park ground.

We used to drink non-alcoholic 'hop bitters' in a place called Fred's Tavern and once a week we'd go to the Palaise de Dance in the town centre.

When Carl left Bolton to join Preston North End, we did not see one another for the best part of nine years, but what a surprise I got one night up at Barnsley.

I was playing for the English League X1 against the Irish League selection. It was a night game up at Oakwell around 1970. I arrived at the ground with my mate Mike Summerbee from Manchester City and we get a look at the match programme and the Irish centre-forward is down as C. Davenport. Mike says to me: "Well there can only be one of them ! And how right he was!

Carl, I hope the book goes well for you and I hope I get a complimentary copy after looking after you so well all those years ago at Bolton. All the best.

Francis Lee. (Bolton Wanderers, Manchester City & England)

BILLY GEORGE INTRODUCTION

The late 1960s and '70s represented a Golden Age in Cork football, a time when Cork Hibernians and Cork Celtic competed for top billing on Leeside. The value of genuine competition was never more graphically illustrated as the two local rivals vied with one another for the major championships in the League of Ireland. And the fans rolled up in their thousands to enjoy the quality of the football that was played and to revel in the successes that were achieved.

There were many, of course, who contributed to this vibrant scene, many who played their part in bringing the Cork clubs to the level where they were able to win the major trophies and rub shoulders with some of Europe's top teams in the former European Cup, Cup-Winners Cup and Fairs Cup competitions.

It was a joyous time when local fans flocked to Flower Lodge and Turner's Cross to celebrate the exploits of successive teams powered by the best of local talent and a conveyor belt of talented imported professional players from England. This policy of enhancing local teams with selected players from the English League has long been a tradition in Cork football, stretching back to the 1950s when the late, great Raich Carter started the trend with Cork Athletic.

The continuing success of Hibs and Celtic meant the demand for new players was always keen. And while Cork fans will recall with pride the impact and ability of many talented imports, there is no disputing that one of their number - Carl Davenport - made a bigger impression than most.

Carl will always figure large in everybody's memory of those years. Football fans glory most of all in the exploits of those players who make a career of scoring goals and Carl etched his name in the history of Cork football by scoring lots of goals, many of them spectacular goals.

His exploits on the field of play were extravagant, his goals exhilarating. He proved, week after week, that he could score against the best defences for he was effective off either foot and was also a powerful header of the ball. His goal-scoring talent helped him win all of the major honours in Irish football with Celtic and with Hibs and led to his selection on several occasions on the League of Ireland representative team.

His football career began while he was still a schoolboy and he spent time with Bolton Wanderers, Preston North End, Wigan Athletic, Stockport County and, finally, Macclesfield Town before he made the move that helped him fulfill his potential when he transferred to Cork City in 1967.

Carl's impact on the Cork football scene was immediate and his barnstorming, swashbuckling, style of play meant that he quickly assumed the status of a Superstar on Leeside. Long before Multi-channel TV brought the glitz and glamour of the international professional game into our living-rooms, Cork could boast of having a living legend in the person of Carl Davenport who gloried in the attention his football exploits attracted and capitalised upon his status to live life to the full.

The fact is that Carl Davenport's name will forever be recalled in Cork as often for his activities off the field as on it, for he was a superstar by nature as well as by reputation. "The Dav" - as he was known - was the subject of debate as much for his nocturnal activities, for his social transgresses - whether real or imagined - as he was for his goal-scoring exploits. And his happy-go-lucky nature meant he enjoyed the exaggerated stories that surrounded his private life too much to attempt to discount them.

"The Dav" was a real, genuine, character who lived for today and found the perfect home for his talents and preferred lifestyle in Cork. His story is an unusually entertaining one in consequence and extraordinarily so, given his strict upbringing in Bolton as the only child of two demanding parents.

The pathway that was opened up for him by his football talent took him on a journey that was never predictable, never dull. On the way he befriended many colleagues some who went on to win World Cup medals - many associates and contemporaries who enriched his life and contributed to a story that is far from ended.

"The Dav" now lives in Bolton and he retains a keen interest in Irish football and in Cork to where he returns regularly for some spiritual nourishment. He has decided to commit his story to paper in response to repeated entreaties to do so from his many friends and it is sure to provide a fascinating insight into one of the most memorable periods in Irish sport.

THE EARLY YEARS

THE cobble stoned streets and terraced houses of Farnworth in the north-west of England was where I was born on May 30th, 1944. The town is just 20 minutes drive from Bolton but a world away in another sense.

We had 14 terraced houses on either side of the street - Charles Street - and two big gas lamps. A man would light them using a big, long pole when it was going dark and put them out again early in the morning - at first light. There were hundreds of streets like mine and we all lived in houses that had two rooms downstairs and three upstairs!

There was no bathroom in those hardy days and the toilet was outside in the backyard next to the coal shed. Believe it or not ... Charles Street is still a cobbled street to this day!

In the harsh winter months, we'd have a night light or a candle near the water pipes to prevent them freezing over and inside the house, we'd have real coal fires in the two downstairs rooms. We didn't know what central heating was, to be honest. Most streets in those days had a pie shop on the corner which is hard to believe and there were chip shops aplenty in my home place. All the people who lived in those cobbled streets knew one another and you were never short of company. You didn't need to lock your front door at night and it was a very safe world back then. It was like one big happy family in Farnworth in the 1940s and 50s. The main road in Farnworth was called Market Street and it was full of small privately owned shops from butchers to cobblers and my parents owned one shop 'Davenport's Hardware' and they sold everything from fireguards to rubbing or 'donkey' stones - they were used to keep the front door steps of the houses clean and tidy. The saying in those days was that if you had a clean front door step, you had a clean house!

Carl at just four years old with his mother Hilda, his American cousin Frankie
from Rhode Island and his dad Jim at Farnworth Park near Bolton in 1948.
Jim played with Blackburn Rovers in midfield during the War years.

Carl on Blackpool Promenade, aged 9, with his parents Jim and Hilda.

Buckets and Spades in Newquay!
Carl, aged 4, on summer holiday with his parents in southern England.

A studio photograph of Carl, aged 14, in his local Farnwoth Boys Club green
and white hooped gear. Farnworth were all-conquering at schoolboy level
in the Bolton area in the 1950's and several of the team,
including Carl went on to play professionally at Bolton Wanderers, Preston
North End, Stockport, Wigan & Macclesfield Town.

14

There was no shortage of public houses either where cards, dominoes and darts were played and they were usually played in a small room to the rear of the pub called 'the snug' and just off the main bar. The stories and characters in there were great. Quite near our house was a small railway station and a big hotel called the Rawson Arms. It had 60 bedrooms and was built in the 19th century to accommodate railway passengers coming and going to Manchester and on to London. We also had a canal close to the family home and the barges would come and go with shipments of coal and any other material bound for Manchester. It was a 100 mile stretch of waterway and was always bustling and busy. At one time, the post was even delivered by boat.

In Farnworth, in the old days, we were lucky enough to have five cinemas: the Savoy, the Ritz, Palace, Empire and Hippodrome. That was a lot for such a small town but they too were always full and busy places with two shows a night. I was in a queue one night at the Hippodrome and it was 400 yards long - the film was *Rock Around the Clock* starring Bill Haley and the Comets. This film in and around 1955 started the ' rock and roll' craze in Britain and I was 10 or eleven at the time and very much wanted to be a footballer. Even on the way to the cinema in those days, I'd be kicking a tennis ball along the way. I loved that little ball. It was about this time that I joined Farnworth Boys Club which was only down the road from me at a place called Moses Gate.

Alan Ball's father used to say to people in Sweden where he coached for a spell, if you have never heard of Moses Gate, you have never lived. When young Alan was manager of Manchester City, we would go into his office after a game, Vince, Bally's right-hand man, would say as soon as he saw me and my pal: "Here they come MGM and he'd pause and

15

then say: "Moses Gate Mafia" and the place would be in uproar. That is where I started to play my football with the Boys Club and we had a team in the Bolton Boys Federation and our home pitch was at All Saints School which was just around the corner from the club. Did I say pitch? Naw, there was no grass on it in those days, it was just cinders. A sliding tackle and you could end up losing your leg. My pal Francis Lee played for Winrows, a team from Westhoughton, which was another suburb of Bolton. We won the league and the cup in our first season and I bagged a record 84 goals - scoring 10 in one match against Morris's of Edgeworth - their ground belonged to the local school too and is supposed to be the oldest pitch in the world or the most dangerous pitch in the world...!

About six months after playing those games against each other, Francis and I joined Bolton Wanderers and started our professional careers together. We have been friends ever since and we still pal around together to this day - over 50 years - imagine that ! Nowadays there are no gas lamps, coal fires or outside toilets in Farnworth but I will let you decide if you think things are better or worse today. I personally think they are worse, even if I do have champagne and cheese in my fridge.

As I say, I was brought up in Farnworth. My father Jim and mother Hilda and myself made up my family, I was an only child.

From an early age, Dad taught me how to kick a ball with both feet, and head balloons in the house. Our next door neighbour bought me my first football size 3, leather.

Mrs Beckett was the old lady's name. My father was a glazier by trade; he worked for a leaded light company, putting stain glass windows in churches.

Later they bought that hardware shop, it was a lock up shop (did not live there) on the main street, opening hours 9am – 6pm except Sundays.

I was about eight years old at this stage and when I came home from school, I would do some house work, set the table and make the fire, if I didn't I would be in trouble with my mother, as she gave me a hard time all my life.

Things were never good between us, she pushed too hard, and I could never please her.

Later in life I must say, it must have done me some good as I am now a perfectionist. My house is always immaculate and I insist on ironing and looking after my clothes. So after I had done my jobs, out with the ball, hours of kicking a tennis ball, any sort of ball, against a wall, garage door, a lamp post, or on those old back street cobbles or pavements, no problem except when our ball went over somebody's wall and into their back garden.

I would go out after dark in the street, under the lamp; a goal would be if we hit the lamp post, now they can't hit the goal, never mind the post.

As time went on football scouts started to watch my progress as a goal scorer, by the time I was 14, club managers were always at my house, but my mother was still a dominant person and wouldn't let me sign for any of them, as she wanted me living at home.

My parents turned down thousands of pounds from some top clubs in England.

After a time it came down to Manchester City and Bolton Wanderers, where I could live at home. I signed for Manchester City, illegally, as I was still at school.

So months passed, I was ready for leaving school at 14 years old.

The headmaster, Mr. Ormaston called me into his office, and told me he had found out that I had signed forms for City. In his next breath, he told me it was illegal, and that if I did not sign for Bolton Wanderers, it could go to court. He had been got at, so Bolton it was, no thousands of pounds, just an old training ball.

My Mum said we are not selling our son, to play with a football ... how naive but that's how parents were back then.

I started at Bolton Wanderers on £5 per week, first team £20, but that was good money for a lad then. I would give my wages to my parents every week, they gave me my spending money, two shillings and six pence.

I thought that was fine at the time, I could go to the Bolton 'Palaise' and have a good night out, with my pal Francis Lee, where there was great music and plenty females.

I was not making enough headway at Bolton in the two years I was there, leading goal-scorer every season, but I had the likes of the great Nat Lofthouse at centre-forward in the first team, so I was still down the pecking order.

At 17, I moved to Preston North End, who had been trying to sign me as a boy. I did great at Preston, scoring goals for the reserves and I made a couple of first team appearances.

Tom Finney was still playing then, so I had learned a lot at these two clubs, by training with two of the greatest players of all time, both great headers of goals, and Tom, with as much skill, ball control and dribbling skills as the legendary George Best. That's some statement.

I got impatient again and asked for a transfer and Stockport County bought me, good money £30 per week, on a two-year contract, but they knew I had plenty of potential and I nearly went to Tottenham Hotspurs, for a club record fee.

But the negotiations broke down. I wonder if my mother had

anything to do with it as I would have had to live in London. You never know!

When I went to Preston my parents bought me a car, a brand new Ford Cortina, WBN 678. This make of car had not been out long. They had bought it out of my money, they were still giving me a little spending money and by this time, it was women and more women, so I was spending more and more.

Stockport County got into financial trouble and still are to this day. But they were wild days.

I went to Wigan next where I broke all goal-scoring records - me and my striking partner Harry Lyons, scored over a 100 goals between us and the team won everything.

Ralph Gubbins, who was at Bolton with me, was at Wigan when I arrived, he had scored two goals in the FA Cup semi-final for Bolton and had put them in the Wembley final against Manchester United, but did not play as Nat Lofthouse who had been injured in the semi-final was declared fit.

Despite all the money my parents had saved for me, through handing over my wages every week, I was still on next to nothing spending money. It was ridiculous and forced me into gambling to live like the rest of the players.

My mother and father did not believe in banks, so I knew my money was in the house somewhere. After months of searching, I was in the bath one day and I noticed the bath panel, which was glass, and at the end of it was another small panel, with four silver topped heads in the screws, I wonder what's in there I thought?

I unscrewed these silver tops, put my hand inside the hole, it felt like a large, old fashioned biscuit tin, pulled it out, large elastic bands were around it, took them off, opened the lid, and bingo ... there was my money, all in £100 bundles, in total four and-a-half thousand pounds.

Farnworth Boys' Club Junior Football Team in 1957-58 season.
Back Row Left to right;Eric Green (Manager), Billy Charston, Barry Tumblety, Trevor Hadfield,
Jack Penny, Bob Standring, David Hatton. Front Row Left to Right; Terry Mann, Tom Lawrence,
Carl Davenport, Ernie Machin, Albert Ashworth and Norman Green

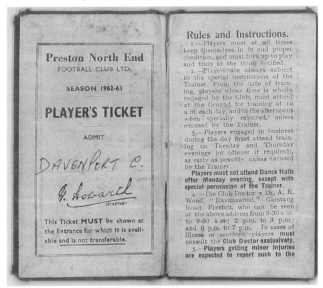

Carl's Players Ticket for Preston North End
Season 1962-63

I took £10 pounds, then £50 and this went on for 18 months. Before long it was all gone. All that time, every night, I would come home expecting the worst and that my folks had found the biscuit tin empty.

It was the worst time of my life, the waiting, one night about 11.30pm I arrived home and my parents were in bed, I shouted upstairs as I always did: "I am home now". Mother shouts: "Your Dad wants to talk to you, he's coming downstairs, and if I were him I would kill you," she had not changed . My dad, like the gentleman he was, never once raised his voice to me.

He said: "Well son, what did you spend the money on?"

I said, "Horses, women and drink".

He said: "Promise me you will never back horses again," I said "Ok but what about the women and drink?" Well I will tell you this, what a relief in a way, that I had been found out, the weight had been lifted, like my Dad said, "You have been punished every night for 18 months, wondering if we'd found the money, that was punishment enough for anybody," and he was spot on.

So it was a new start at home, and a new start with a fresh club. I left Wigan after one season and 48 goals and joined Macclesfield Town, bitter rivals of Wigan and met up with my best pal, Billy Myerscough, who had won an FA Cup winners medal with Aston Villa when they beat Manchester United in the final.

Northern Ireland international, Peter McFarland scored the winning goal for Villa, and in later years, he was to become manager of Glentoran and wanted to sign me from Cork Hibernians.

I was now playing for Macclesfield Town, but after all this, I was still, yes still living at home and Mother still on my back – no getting away?

My first season. We win everything, League Championship, Cups, the lot.

Wigan third place, I scored 57 goals, fantastic. The season after was 1966-67, by January I had scored 51 goals, and along came Cork Celtic to buy me and the rest as they say is history.

Why did I go to Ireland?

Basically to get away from my mother. She had held me back too long, and the relief, I cannot describe it. I remember leaving that day for Cork and I hadn't a clue where I was going, but I was free, and that most likely sounds terrible. I have never told this story to anybody before, I have been too embarrassed and ashamed, I have never stolen, cheated, or told lies in my life, people like me for my straight-talking and honesty, so I have been puzzled by this event all through my life.

The moral of this story is don't push your children too hard, give them the amount of spending money that is right with the times, and don't make them cry, if they have scored four or five goals like I did, don't harp on and on about the two bloody tap-ins I missed.

My mother was just never satisfied with her son.

My mother passed away about five years later, they would visit me in Ireland, and I would send cuttings of the match reports from the *Cork Examiner* and Cork *Evening Echo* to Farnworth every Monday.

Then I'd come home for two months in the summer when I wasn't playing with the close season.

After mother died, my father came over for a month at a time, he was the best dad, I loved him so much, and he was so pleased that I ended up in Cork.

The youngest player-manager, at 23, to ever manage a club. I got to know him really well in a way I hadn't really known him as a boy, but this was great, having a drink with my Dad and the team after a game in Cork.

I had never had a drink with him before, and had never sworn in front of him. We are in the pub with the lads after the game, The Market Bar, after a few pints. They called him Mr. Dav, they started F'ing and blinding, my Dad never flinched. I was amazed, you don't think your Dad's ever going to hear talk like that, but of course they do.

Dad died two years after my mother and I miss him so much to this day. He taught me all the skills of a footballer, even how to dress, and be civil and polite to people.

My Dad would say to me once you get behind the glass you're made for life. He meant the television screen. He had many great anecdotes or sayings: Someone has to be the best, so it might as well be you!

So whoever you play football against they only have two arms and two legs like you. He was eating out one day and they had added a salad to his meal, he said he didn't like lettuce, it grows too near the ground.

When you shoot at goal and keep the ball very low, he always called it a daisy-cutter, and he said I can tell a good player by the way he laces and ties his boots, I don't know if that is right. The best one was, he told me to always play the one nearest to you, I thought he meant, play the ball to the nearest man, or make a play for the lady who was nearest, after a couple of thousand girls I found out what he meant. I was at his funeral, in the church yard around the grave, my Old Auntie, says Jim (my Dad), always said play the one nearest to you, my ears pricked up, then she said you know love he was a good Domino player. Ha, ha.

Me being the only child, as my parents were 40 when I arrived, as they had lost Victor, their first born, at six months, and it would have been great to have had a brother. When my Mum and Dad died in the space of two years, it was a bad time for me, I was on my own. There were no brothers or sisters to turn to so it was all down to me.

Let me explain. My Dad Jim, was the youngest of eleven children, three boys, the rest girls, one brother George who was the eldest in the family, had one son, but he never had children, the other brother Wilfred, had a son called Harry, but he died aged 11. So there was only me to keep the 'Davs' going. What pressure!

I have two sons, Mark and Jason, two fantastic lads, but so far they have only produced lovely girls, yes I am a Granddad (but keep it quiet), and my daughter Samantha had a baby girl, Chyna , so she is only half a 'Dav'. I do love them all deeply, and they were the best thing, ever to happen to me, I am so proud of them, the boys live in America and my daughter lives in Bolton, We plan trips and holidays together, and are very close to each other, which is very important to me.

When my father was 15, he worked down the pit, you had a choice in those days, the pit or go to war against Germany. What a choice in life? His job was a blacksmith, shoeing the pit ponies, which were used to carry the coal or pull coal trucks. We don't realise just how lucky we are today.

He was a very dry but funny man, he told me a story one day, that an Irishman called Paddy, can you believe that, started work one Monday morning. In his first day, the man in charge gave Paddy instructions, and a map, showing all these tunnels down the mines, and where to start digging for coal, and said, to be back at ground level, after 12 hours down the mine.

Well Paddy did appear, but 24 hours later, his boss was waiting for him, all concerned. He says to Paddy: "Do you realise that we are at war with Germany? Paddy says: "No wonder ... we're pinching their coal."

I remember going on holidays to Scotland with my parents, and aunt and uncle, who were quite well off, as they had a gown shop, and always had classy cars, mostly Jaguars, and in the early 50s this was unheard of, and more to the point, there were not many cars on the road in those days.

In Scotland there was beautiful scenery, and lakes, but it can get pretty remote in the highlands, so we were driving along, and we get a puncture in the back tyre. In those days, they had an inner tube inside, so that meant they had to jack the car up, take the wheel off, and put a patch on the tube.

The uncle gets the tin with the puncture essentials, glue, patches, sandpaper, but there was only one patch, no problem, they had sanded the inner tube where the hole was, put the glue on the patch. Uncle says, pass me the patch Jim. The patch could not be found, gone, disappeared into thin air.

My father decides to walk to the nearest village, buy a new outfit, but it was five miles away, and in bad weather.

The Scottish call it 'a light mist', anywhere else in the world it's known as rain.

He arrives back three hours later, opens the tin, puts the glue on the patch, kneels down and puts the patch over the hole. What's stuck to the sole of his shoe, yes you've guessed it, the missing bloody patch. 10 miles walk in the rain, all of us freezing in the car, and Dad got it stuck on the bottom of his shoe, all the time.

MY FIRST FOOTBALL & THE 'BIG O'

I used to go the cinema twice a week with my Mum and Dad, in Farnworth. We would go on a Wednesday and Saturday. The first showing would be at 5pm, the second showing at 8.30pm. It was great, into the toffee shop next door, where my mother would get a load of toffee and at the interval, ice cream.

The films in those days had a different feel about them. Roy Rodgers, his wife Dale Evans and, of course, Trigger.

Another famous cowboy at the time was Gene Autrey and his wonder horse: 'Champion'. They were great times. I would think nothing of getting on my bike with a couple of pals, lunch in our saddle bags, and cycle to Southport for the day.

It was only 30 miles but I would not like to try it now. At this age, I was a member of Bolton Harriers, where I was coached to run faster, with style, and to jump longer, which in latter years was very useful to me, all my life, the women loved it !

We played a lot of street games in those days, marbles, hop scotch, kick-out ball. We would put cotton thread around somebody's door knocker, we would hide, pull the cotton, the owner would come out but nobody there, mischievous things of young boys, it's still more fun than sitting on your arse playing PlayStation. Technology has a lot to answer for.

Farnworth was a lovely small town. I was three before I could remember anything, my Grandma bought me a three wheeler bike.

That was special then, but on my fourth birthday our neighbour next door, old Mrs Beckett bought a size 3 FOOTball which was leather, from that day I would play in the cobbled street 'till it went dark. I and a few pals would kick a tennis ball against a lamp post. If you hit the lamp post it was a goal, we would dribble each other, and take a shot at it. We would play under the street lights until our parents shouted for us to go in but then we had no television or PlayStation in those days.

I would have been world champion at PlayStation if I had spent the same time as I did practising my football skills. God! I am glad I was born when I was, I would have missed being brought up properly by my parents.

They made me dust and Hoover, run errands, be polite and not to talk back to older people and to be respectful and caring of the older generation.

All this got me ready for life at 12-13 when I left Junior school at 11 in my last year we won Lunchtime Schools 11 and under for St. John's. It's never been done since, what a team.

My most enjoyable time as a young lad was probably around the age of 12-15, spending money, 10 bob (50p new money) for the week, go to the cinema on Saturday night, then go to a local fish and chip shop, chips, steak-pudding and peas, a slice of bread, cup of tea, in the eating area at the back of the shop. Two shillings (10p) with my pals.

Great music in the late 50s, Eddie Cochran, *Summer Time Blues*, Lonnie Donnegan, *Putting on the Style*, Bobby Vee, *Take Good Care of My Baby*, Buddy Holly, Johnny Preston and my favourite the Big O himself, Roy Orbison, *Only the Lonely*, Running Scared", *Pretty Woman*, fantastic music.

Bill Furey, *Halfway to Paradise*, Perry Como. Del Shannon, and many more.

They were some of the happiest days of my life.

THE VERNON GIRLS

The great Lester Piggott, Ed Moses, Cassius Clay, Stanley Matthews (my hero), Len Hutton (cricket), Emile Zatopek (athletics).

They were legends of their time, they would just have been as good today if not better, as they were all ahead of their time.

I remember one Saturday tea-time, I was watching a *Top of the Pops* kind of show, it was called *Oh Boy.* I was about 14 years old. The TV was in our front room, my parents were in the kitchen two doors away, one was a sliding door, and on the show every week was a female group called the Vernon Girls, they had the tightest fitted hot pants you have ever seen. I had by this time pulled a small padded stool up to the TV and about a foot away from the screen. I would have got into the telly if I could. So turned on was I by these gorgeous Vernon Girls that I started to play with myself, getting carried away, I had not heard my mother open the sliding door and then the other door, obviously she thought I was up to something.

Suddenly there she was in the front room, "What do you think you are doing?" I was speechless, caught in the act. She then says, "You want to be a professional footballer, you can forget that, you know what that does to you?" "No", my reply, "Your bones will turn to chalk", I thought, Oh my God, I am going to end up on a blackboard. It never happened again, I bought a lock for the door (only joking).

My Dad was still out in the kitchen and mother must have hand signalled to him to what I was doing, because I did not hear her speak. Dad, then said, "Hilda, you should respect his privacy, and don't be creeping around the house."

It was never mentioned again, but that chalk, did frighten me for a while. But in later life, it didn't stop me having over two thousand birds, and I did not have any aviary!

Where did things change in living? I would, say mid 70s and not for the best, kids started being lazy and fat. I hate fat people, why? They don't have any respect for themselves, couch potatoes, all they do is eat and drink in excess, and watch TV.

So if these people have grown into the habit, their kids go the same way, and with less discipline, so what chance have we got as to getting this country back to how it used to be, with all children slim, through sports and going on walks, instead of causing damage, litter and showing no respect for others.

In the past every house had clean windows and everybody's front door step was spotless. People would rub their step with a special stone, and then colour it with another one, either white or cream. If you did not have a clean step people would say you had a dirty house.

All neighbours were friends with each other, visiting for a cup of tea and a chat. Every year our street would organise a trip to the Illumination at Blackpool by Charabang (coach) they were great days.

They will never come back, because people only care about themselves now, and nobody else. Sad.

GROWING

When I started kicking a ball about, I was four years old. My Dad had been good at the game, as he played for Blackburn Rovers for a spell during the War years and he trained and taught me everything all through my early football days.

After junior school, where they won their first ever football trophy, and never won one since, I went to Harper Green, a school for girls and boys aged from 11-15. Girls in one half of the school and boys in the other. When examination times came around, I would get good marks at Geography, English and Woodwork, but it was at Sports I excelled and won medals at running, that's sprinting (I was useless at cross-country), cricket, tennis and, of course, football.

I would play football for the school team on Saturday mornings and for Farnworth Boys Club in the afternoons, both Under 14, and in between I would go home for my dinner, which consisted of a meat pie and potatoes, then change my football boots and off again with a clean, dry pair, and in one season for the two teams, I scored 178 goals.

This sort of goal-scoring ratio attracted the attention of club scouts, who would be waiting for me outside school, and top managers who would be at my house, sitting in our front room when I got home from school.

Famous people like Sir Matt Busby from Manchester United, Stan Cullis at Wolverhampton Wanderers and George Poyser at Manchester City, to name a few.

Farnworth Boys Club, played in the Bolton Boys Federation, where a lot of star players started, and we were a good team, six of that team went on to play professional football for various clubs, that shows how good this team were, we won the League and Cup that season, our nearest challengers, were a team called Winrows, a team from just outside Bolton.

A blonde-haired lad played for them, his name Francis Lee, and he wasn't half bad. His last club was England.

We both joined Bolton Wanderers the following season on the same day and we have been friends ever since.

On Saturday mornings before I signed for Bolton Wanderers, myself, Dad and a goalkeeper called Albert Lord, would go and practice on this football pitch near our house, and I would keep shooting as hard as I could, with both feet, for a good two hours, I improved and so did he, even with concussion, never liked goalkeepers.

One Sunday, I had a little red-haired lad centering balls for me, to hit first time towards goal, and also to head these crosses. These crosses were not up to standard for me, but after a few weeks he improved, and so did the goalkeeper, and the little fellow also signed for Bolton 12 months later, yes, it was Alan Ball, World Cup winner in 1966, you have to start somewhere.

So I signed for Bolton Wanderers at 15 years of age. My first day, I arrive and in I go through the main entrance, I turn right, but see the lush green pitch first, then into the long dressing room, I walk in head down, hoping nobody would notice me, out of the corner of my eye I see the great Nat Lofthouse, the Lion of Vienna, as he is known, and some other internationals as well were getting changed to go training.

So I see a free hook to hang my clothes on, and start to get changed, just then the Bolton left-back walks in, he's just returned from England duty, with the World Cup squad in Sweden, and Tommy Banks was not somebody to mess with.

He spoke in an old Lancashire accent and loud, and had played for Bolton from being a young lad. My worst nightmare was going to take place on my first day. He comes up to me and says: Do you know that's my hook, I said sorry, he says I have that hook since it was a nail.

Off I went, clothes under my arm, shoes in my hand, and asked if there was a spare hook, which nobody had owned since it was a nail.

There were six ground staff, young lads like myself, they call them apprentice professionals today, and when you turn 17, you became a full professional. My pal Francis Lee was one of them. We would train every morning with the rest of the professionals. In the afternoon for a couple of hours we would do odd jobs, cleaning boots or rolling the grass. After matches on Saturday, we would sweep the stands, clear off the litter, beer bottles, whatever had been left behind after the games.

I remember one Monday morning, that was the day when there was no training for anybody, the only players present that day were people with injuries who were having treatments. Well this particular morning, we were sweeping under the huge stand, where there were Beer Bars, toilets etc, old Frank a member of the cleaning staff, a nice man but very deaf, we decided we would have a bit of fun.

He would drink anything, believe me. So we find this empty bottle of Brown Ale, we then piss in the bottle, and put a top on it. We climb up on the roof of the toilets, for a better view of our hero, and the new bottle of beer, we see him with his brush, shovel and bin bag and as he picks every bottle up, he checks them, then his eyes light up, he's seen the full one, he picks it up, opens it and drinks it down in one, off he goes looking for more, how we did not fall off the top of the toilets, laughing I just don't know.

We were always playing tricks, but one day it all back-fired on us.

Francis Lee's job was to keep the changing rooms clean and the large bath that fitted 12 players in at once, and the showers and toilets. He would clean the tiles in the bath, then hose the pipes down with this powerful jet spray. Well one day I went to use the toilet in the bathroom, one of four, Francis saw me go in the end one, I thought I knew what he was thinking, so I slid underneath and into the next one, he must have turned around to turn the hose pipe on, and had missed seeing some person go into the one which he thought I was in. All of a sudden, I hear this mad rush of water from this pipe, and he had put it over the top of this toilet. He's laughing his head off, just then this voice shouts: "What the fuck is going on," - it was only the gaffer (manager) Mr. Bill Ridding, a strict disciplinarian.

My time at Bolton did not last long after that, but I was the club's leading goal scorer for two seasons, in the club's colts team and 'A' team.

I got a hat-trick against Manchester United 'A' team. I only found out a few years ago, from my pal Alan Ball who played in the same game that George Best, our other pal, played for United that day.

Carl in 1961 in Preston North End youth team (second from right - back row)
Also in the team photo is Frank Clarke (Newcastle & Notts Forest) 3rd from left in back row.

Carl at a Preston North End training session at Deepdale with Howard Kendall
(ex-Everton & Manchester City) fifth from the right
and first team coach George Barge (RIP)

The Dav's goal celebration after he scored one of his 48 league
& FA Cup goals for Wigan Athletic.
Picture Courtesy of Evening Post & Chronicle, Wigan

An airborne 'Dav' playing for for Maccesfield rounds the Moseley keeper only to
see his eventual shot taken off the line by the defender.

THE SWINGING 60's

It was a magic time in the early 60s for beautiful ladies, mini skirts, new make-up and hairstyles. Also new dance crazes, such as the Twist, Locomotion and Jive.

In Bolton at this time everybody went to this famous Palaise de Dance Ballroom, it's a fantastic dance floor, and stage, upstairs a balcony which you could walk all the way around, a great view of the ladies dancing, where you could pick out the one you fancied.

Spoiled for choice most of the time, but there was always next week. I was playing for Bolton Wanderers in those days, and my pal Francis Lee, would be with me on those great nights out.

In those days, it was just soft drinks that were served in dance halls. I remember after training, we would go for our lunch, to Joe's café, across from Burnden Park (Bolton's ground).

It was paid for by the club. After lunch, as we finished training for the day, we would go to Little Fred's Temperance Bar, which was next door to the café, we would order Sasperala, Dandelion and Burdock, - non-alcoholic as that's what temperance means, that's for people under 40, who don't know what it means - Ha! Ha!

We would then take our drinks upstairs where we had a full-size snooker table. We would play for the rest of the afternoon, sometimes joined by other footballers, but mostly just the two of us. He was not a bad player, but he struggled if I did not take the triangle off the reds at the start of the game.

Francis lives in Wimslow now, on the outskirts of Manchester, he has his own snooker table, and still plays. It was at this time that he started a small business of his own collecting waste paper, and recycling it, which was not as popular as it is today. Well he kept at it, and after 20 years he had one of the

36

biggest corporations in Britain making kitchen and toilet rolls.

The moral of this story, he started at the bottom and finished at the bottom and in between made himself into a multi-millionaire. Well done, Franny.

In later years, I started selling his toilet rolls around the Blackpool area, where there are thousands of guest houses and hotels, a perfect way to make money, and I did very well at this, being a good talker and listener.

One particular hotel, the Imperial on the sea front, in I went, suited up, and looking smart, up to reception, and asked if I could see the buyer. Out he comes and I explain what I am selling. Immediately he says, "We use Izal." I say, "Izal, that's the most dangerous toilet paper you could use," "Why is that," he replied, "Well Izal is a very tough and slippery paper and it's a well known fact, that a lot of times, it slips off your bottom and slides up your back."

Before he could speak, I said, "Ours is so soft it's a pleasure to get diarrhoea." I got the order, a big one at that, and off I went with a big smile on my face.

I still play snooker to this day, once a week in Bolton, with a few of my old football pals. Charlie Cooper, a left-back with Bolton who then became a traffic policeman. How he kept the job I will never know, as he never booked anybody as he worked in his own town of Farnworth.

In fact myself and Charlie went to the same school. He also played soccer for them, as I did later. He is two years older than me, but we were at school the same time. My other pal who plays snooker with us, and also played for Bolton with me, is Freddie Hill, he also played for England and was a genius with the ball and the most unassuming person you will ever meet. We have known each other 50 years.

*The Dav with Groundsman and Alan Ball Senior (First team coach)
at Stoke City in 1968-69*

BOLTON – BLACKPOOL TRAIN

When I played for Preston North End, my pal Bally was at Blackpool, and as we were both from Bolton, we would catch the same train in the morning. I would get off at Preston, Alan would carry on to Blackpool, another 15 minutes further down the track.

This particular Friday, before I got off he says, "Wish I was you," as I was a regular on the reserve team, he was playing for the fifth team, Blackpool Juniors.

A couple of hours later after training, as footballers only do light training the day before a match, I was again waiting for the return of the Blackpool train at Preston station. Just as the train arrives at the platform and I get to see this little red head, hanging out of the window, shouting, "I am in the first team at Liverpool tomorrow!" What happened?

There had been four injuries in the team's higher than what

38

Alan was playing in, can you believe he was wishing he was me, two hours before, he never looked back after that.

Five years later he plays in the winning World Cup team, which beat Germany at Wembley.

On one of those train journeys coming back to Bolton, there were no corridors or toilets on most trains, just single compartments.

I wanted to take a leak. I opened the window with the big leather strap, and had one out the window. I was lucky, because a train was flashing past the opposite way, and I nearly ended up with a dick full of door handles !

When I signed for Preston North End, the great Tom Finney was playing for them. He had played for England in every forward line position. Two-footed and a great header of the ball, the perfect footballer.

At that time they had a great team, Frank O'Farrell, who was from Cork, Johnny Fulham, who later played with Shamrock Rovers, and Alan Kelly goalkeeper, who went on to manage the Irish international team. I signed professional forms for them in 1961, and was there for a few years.

The manager was a Cliff Britton, who had been a great player himself. After a couple of seasons, I decided a pay rise was due, as I'd been scoring plenty of goals, so I plucked up the courage to go and see him.

So down the corridor I went. I knock on the door, "Come in," was the reply. "Yes, what can I do for you"? "I think I should be on more money and would like a pay rise Mr Britton. He looked at me and I froze on the spot. "Why?" he says.

"Well, I have been playing well and scoring goals." "Yes, I know that," he said. Then I come out with a remarkable statement, "Tom Finney is on more money than me." "He's a lot better player than you!" What could I say to that, after a short pause, I replied, "He's not in the summer season." You see in the summer season we did not play and players were on less wages in the off-season, so he was only as good as me. I did get the pay rise, only because he said, "I was a cheeky little fecker."

When playing for Preston, who are one of the oldest clubs in the Football League, after home games, a few of us would go for a drink or two. Then on to a nightclub.

We would have our club blazers on with the PNE badge on the top pocket, as it was a compulsory thing to wear on match days, and a good pulling power in the night clubs.

When we had a bad night, at 3am, we would get into the car, and drive into the country and park the car in the middle of this large field, and on Sunday morning wake up about 8am.

One of these mornings I awoke, looked through the side window and there was the biggest tongue in the world, it was a cow, it frightened me to death.

By this time we are all hungry, so we drive carefully out of the field, and onto the main road for a couple of miles and, as you know, the only places that are open at that time in the morning are transport cafés, for all night lorry drivers, and this one's name is Dirty Dicks, but because it was Sunday, I used to call it Unclean Richard's.

After breakfast, we drove back to Preston, a couple of pints in the local pub at dinner time, and then home, knackered, lucky we had Mondays off.

HOW I CAME TO CORK

I had played in all the divisions and was at Macclesfield Town. I had just broken the club's goal-scoring record with 58 goals.

The season before with Wigan Athletic I was the leading goal-scorer with 48, thus winning my second championship medal in two seasons with different clubs.

Alan Ball Snr. was coach at Stoke City. He sent his son, Alan over to my house. It was only 10 minutes away. That was 1966 and six months previously, Alan had won a World Cup medal with England.

Ball senior's message, relayed through his son, was to ask me if I would be interested in going to Ireland to play in Cork and would I let him know as soon as possible.

I gave him my answer a week later and Cork Celtic bought me from Macclesfield Town. But what I did not know was that Alan's dad had told Celtic a very unusual thing.

He told them they were getting someone who would get them a goal a game and was also a bit of a playboy of the Western World, all rolled into one.

Events were to prove that was indeed what they had got.

I was offered terms of £45 per week and another £45, total £90 per week, until they got me a job, which never happened.

John Horgan, a director, did once try to find employment for me and actually lined-up an interview. He told me he had been talking to Joe O'Reilly, a friend of his over a few drinks.

I went for the interview at the arranged time of 11am one Monday morning to Joe O' Reilly's, travel agency on the Western Road. It was not far away from where I lived on Mardyke Walk, with a lovely family Mr. and Mrs. Dan Hartnett, son Neil and five students, all at university.

I told the receptionist my name and said I had a appointment with Mr. O'Reilly. She went into his office, emerged seconds later and said Mr. O'Reilly would see me but knew nothing about a job.

I thought immediately that Messrs Horgan and O'Reilly must have had more than 'a few drinks'. Joe told me to sit down and we began to talk.

"Did I know anything about horses?" he asked. I said, "I backed a few," not knowing he was talking about his horse-drawn caravans which were situated in Blarney.

But he wanted me to steer or drive them into Cork City, where they were passed on to holiday-makers, for touring around Kinsale and places like that. I asked him how much the job paid. He said: "£12 a week." My reply was I wouldn't get out of bed for that. End of interview with no hard feelings on either side.

I remained on £90 per week as a footballer and I was more than happy with that.

I came over in January, 1967, when both Cork clubs were joint bottom of the league - gates of 200 to 300 people and that's how it all began for me. Not the most glamourous of starts for yours truly.

There had been great players all through the history of Cork football. It was steeped in tradition and had become a sleeping giant which needed waking up.

I well remember my first game. It was of all things the local derby, away at Flower Lodge. We won 2-1. The Celtic team that day in January 1967 was: George Howard, John Clifford, Pat O'Mahony, Ray Cowhie, Eamon Heffernan, Charlie O'Mahony, Sydney Venner, Carl Davenport, Donal Leahy, John 'Blondie' Carroll, Fintan Deegan.

We finished half-way up the league under manager Bill Higgins, who was supposed to have played with one of my old clubs, Bolton Wanderers.

We later discovered that this man who had brought me over to Celtic through Alan Ball was not Bill Higgins, but a pharmaceutical rep, who was trying to get the 'the pill' into Ireland and always had a boot full .

In all honesty, the only positive thing he did was to sign me and I did get a goal a game; 15 in 14 games. Ray Cowhie always called him 'Enry 'Iggins from My Fair Lady.

Come to think of it, he was always after fair ladies! I lived on the Mardyke, as I stated earlier. It was opposite the cricket ground where the Wanderers Cricket team played. I later played for them as a medium pace bowler and won a league medal, with people like Pat Dineen, Paddy Tynan and Danny Duggan, who also played squash with me.

I once arrived back to Cork from England during the summer, parked my car and looked over at a cricket match which was in progress.

I said to a friend of mine that it must have been a very hot couple of months. He said why? I said take a look at the sun tans on that lot fielding. They were a team from Zimbabwe !

That year saw the start of a new job. I was made player/manager, the youngest ever at 23-years-old, and the season was two weeks away.

Training had already started on the sand at Garrettstown, twice a week. Ray Cowhie, Pat O'Mahony, Tony Allen, and all the senior players, were looking in good shape.

For young lads, Paddy Shortt and John Carroll, it was going to be their first season. They were like greyhounds, anyway. No weight and rarin' to go. I had already started a second team as I had a pool of about 36 players. I made Charlie O' Mahony coach, but he also played in the first team squad. He was just

Carl on his debut for Cork Celtic

Carl in the Celtic Colours at Turners Cross

Members of the Cork Celtic team who won the league in 1974,
Front from the left; Alex Ludzic, Charlie O'Mahony Barry Notley, John Blondie Carroll,
Bobby Tambling and Frank O'Neill. Back from left; Paddy Shortt,
Carl Davenport, Gerry Myers, Ben Hannigan, Keith Edwards and Donie Madden

the man I could trust for my reserve team. My secret weapon at the club was my fitness and masseur man, Timmy 'Beckett' Murphy. He was 64 then but was an amazing man, good hands, quick-witted and I thought the world of him.

He used to say to me if you have sex, have egg and bacon after, you will feel perfect again. I must have eaten 10 pigs in 12 months. Joking apart, we once played Rovers at Milltown. We needed a good result, so I asked 'Beckett' what he'd suggest.

He said: "I've got some tablets," and produced a small tin. I instructed him to give them just to the older players but I was whispering and obviously he did not hear me. So he gave everybody one.

Well I did say earlier that Paddy Shortt and John Carroll were like greyhounds. They were now like exocet missiles. To this day, I don't know what these tablets were. They probably were aspirins but they did the trick. We won 2-0 and stayed top of the league.

TImmy Murphy died a few years ago. It was like losing a father. Every Monday after our games, I would pick him up and off we would go for the day out starting at Cissy Young's pub on Magazine Road, on to the airport, Crosshaven's Admiral Drake and the Church Bay Hotel and back to the Market Bar in town. Great times indeed. He had a favourite tipple. In fact, he was adamant that the only way to drink whiskey was with a half of Guinness.

If Beckett said so, who was I to question a man who had been with all the great Cork teams.

He told me about everyone from Florrie Burke to Raich Carter. I was in this pub with him one day and he said, "Do you see that old guy at the bar?" I said "yes." He then said, "When you are at a bar, never say how good you are at anything; because

46

there's always somebody better in every walk of life." The man at the bar was Seanie Mac of Cork Athletic.

In the 1968-69 season, there were great people in the game and great things happening. People were happy with life, the Arcadia, Group Theatre, the Metropole and Kathy Barry's (nightclub) and Slobby Malone, I liked him.

I don't recall a lot about many of the games in which I played for Celtic over three seasons, as a player and player-manager or with Cork Hibernians.

I have League winners' medals with both clubs and was never on a losing team in all 19 local derbies. I think that might be a domestic record or it might just be the luck of the Irish.

I have said that I had some lovely people around me and one such man was the late Donie Forde, secretary of Cork Celtic. He had been in soccer in Cork over 50 years, and had seen many great players and teams.

He did more for the game than anybody I have ever met. His knowledge on-and-off the pitch was incredible. I was so pleased to hear that the main stand at Turner's Cross is named after this lovely man, whom I will always admire.

We played in Sligo one Sunday. It was then the only game we stayed overnight. We set off from Cork the day before at 1pm. My car then was a Zephyr bench seater. The party consisted of Pat O' Mahony, Ray Cowhie, Timmy Murphy (Beckett). Donie Leahy, Tony 'Tucker' Allen and myself.

We had been travelling about an hour when smoke appeared in the car. We stopped and took everything out of the boot, as the skip with all the kit was in there. We couldn't find anything which resembled burning material, after 10 minutes we did find out what was burning. It was Tucker's new suit.

I had been smoking a cigar while driving and had thrown it through the driver's window when it was almost finished,

Tucker was sat right behind me and the cigar had blown back into the car through the window next to him. which he also had open, and into the pocket of his new jacket.

A good start to the journey to Sligo. The other three cars had caught us up by now, so off we headed to our hotel in Sligo, the Imperial, where we always stayed.

After we had our meal, the lads asked if they could have a couple of pints. I said No, not the night before a game, but if you stay close to me and the directors have moved off, just follow me.

I took them to a hotel bar across the river and there was a band playing away.

We had two or three drinks and a couple of our lads got up to sing. (we had great singers). People were looking at us. They knew we were Cork Celtic and I was player-manager. They shouted that we had no chance tomorrow.

We won 3-0 and that shut them up. I got three off Paddy Shortt's crosses into the box. He wasn't drinking. If he had been, he might have got a hat-trick himself. Tony Allen, who has since passed away, was a very good player and a good friend, as were all the team. That's why we were a good team, we all pulled together. Tucker, as we called him, was a little over-weight but very talented. I bought him a sweat suit for training. He used to sweat pints of his favourite tipple (Guinness) at every training session, but never complained, just got on with it.

As I am writing this, I must mention the late John Clifford, a very underrated right-back who always gave his best. A sad end for a very well-liked lad. I never forget nice people, even if I have forgotten most matches, I think I have my priorities right on this one.

The season of 1968-69 we finished joint second, losing out on goal difference, which was a great disappointment to me and the players. I scored 36 goals that season. Just my luck that only 12 months earlier they had stopped the gold watch prize for leading scorer in the country.

The Celtic directors would not buy any new players when the season ended: So I put in my transfer request.

I knew Hibs wanted me. Celtic put a £6,000 price on my head, which was unheard of for a League of Ireland player.

It was a long drawn out transfer saga. Amby Fogarty wanted me badly so I gave my word to him that I would sign for Hibs. I went back home to England for six months. By this time Celtic and Hibs were both paying my wages. It was great. Eventually, Paddy Barry and Ned Trinder, two Celtic directors, came over to see me in Bolton, to raise their offer. But I had given my word to Amby.

It finally got sorted out and I was transferred to Cork Hibs for £3,000, as the league stepped in and halved the fee. It was still a record between two League of Ireland clubs.

My first day back, the season had started, six games had been played. It was a Saturday morning. I went down to Flower Lodge, got into my training gear and went jogging around the pitch. I saw a figure across the pitch. He soon caught up and said: "Are you the Dav I've heard all about? My name is Wiggy". From that day on we were inseparable on-and-off the field.

One night Wiggy and I went out on the town. We ended up in the Carousel, were we met two young ladies.

They asked would we take them home to Crosshaven. I was driving. We got to a bungalow, they got out of the car and walked 20 yards up the garden to the house.

We waited 10 minutes but nobody appeared. I said to Wiggy come on, I'll knock at the front door, which was in the middle of two bay windows. Next thing I heard a loud bang, Wiggy cracked no comment, I grabbed hold of him and pushed him to the ground. Someone in the house was shooting at us with a gun. I had never beaten Wiggy in the 100 yard sprint but I did that night.

Months later, two detective friends of mine who had somehow found out about the incident said a man who lived at the house had been on their wanted list for a long time.

 The Gardai said the man's name was Captain Hegarty and they said they would keep our names out of it when the case went to court. I never took another lady home after that.

I think both Wiggy and I thought it safer to get married, which we did.

Carl Davenport's first port of call in Cork in January 1967 - his first digs at No. 1 Maryville, Mardyke Walk - opposite the Cork County Cricket grounds where he won league medals with Wanderers.

The famous Cork Hibernians team of 1969/70 photographed at Flower Lodge - back row (left to right) - Terry Young, Sonny Sweeney, Martin Sheehan, Joe O'Grady, Alan Aubrey, Carl Davenport, John Brohan, John Lawson. Front Row - (left to right) - Miah Dennehy, Tommy Henderson, Frank Connolly, Noel O'Mahony (capt.), John Herrick, Dave Wigginton and Donie Wallace.

51

Carl as the model professional in a photo shoot for Vogue magazine taken at The Old Thatch Pub in 1969.

Carl with one of his best mates Tommy O'Leary, whose mother ran the Carmelitte Stores near Mardyke Walk. Tommy played rugby for Cork Con in the 1960's and 1970's.

JOHNSON SISTERS & THE SHOWBAND ERA

I was great friends with the Johnson sisters a very popular group around the late 1960s. They had a hit record with "Johnson's Motor Car".

I would always go down to the Munster Arms in Bandon, and strangely enough, that was where I met my pal Wiggy again for the first time a few years ago.

Showbands were great back then, Dickie Rock, Joe Dolan, The Dixies, The Freshmen, Brendan O'Brien etc. etc.

Around Cork there were great places to go, my favourites were Tullagreine House, with the players and their wives. They were good singers as well as being good players.

Donie Leahy and Ray Cowhie would entertain, we had some great nights and mornings.

Other places, like the Midleton dance hall, the Speakeasy at Glenbrook, owned by the Carpenter family, Shandon Boat Club, the Stardust, Group Theatre with Eddie Hayes and Neil Hartnett whose Mum and Dad I was in digs with down the 'Dyke.

Another great pal of mine was Tommy O'Leary, whose parents used to have the Carmelite Stores at the top of the Mardyke. Good times. My local pub in those days was the Western Star, a great character owned the place, the late Derry Crowley or 'Starrie' as he was best known by all the students who went in there from the College.

Derry had been into rugby all his life. He was a nice man, it was Timmy "Beckett" Murphy who introduced me to him. A sportsman through and through. My secret is I love life and people, you cannot beat good company, it's always a pleasure.

I had been doing modelling for Ideal Weatherproofs, a Cork-based company, a lovely man called Gene O'Neill, was one of the main men there, also a good friend of my pal, Ray

Cowhie, and Gene was also a good soccer player himself.

My first job was modelling raincoats outside the Old Thatch in Killeagh and a good-looking girl was also modelling with me .

Roy Hammond was the photographer, a great character, a lovely man, we would eventually socialise a lot, so we decided we would open a night club, on the South Main Street and call it "Back of the Sun" don't ask me how that name came up.

We then started looking for premises, but a friend of ours, Michael Ryan, a reporter at the time wanted part of the action, but we never found the property we wanted.

Roy sadly died and was greatly missed by the people of Cork and Michael Ryan went on to being big on television and 'Nationwide' fame.

Some you win and some you lose. Some of the modelling photographs went into a magazine and 15 years later in Bolton I had a couple of lassies back to my house, and they started yapping about modelling (showing off). I said I did some of that, they looked at me, so I said I'll get the magazine which I had not looked at for some 20 years and not knowing what it was called. Anyway, I finally found it upstairs in a cupboard, so I showed them this, and they were gobsmacked. They opened it up and looked at the photographs, and then informed me this is the top magazine. I say what do you mean, It's Vogue, that's the best. I hadn't a clue, all I was interested in was playing football. It might as well have been the Beano as far as I was concerned.

When with Cork Celtic, we had been playing in Dublin, coming home on the train to Cork, we had our meal, and a few drinks and started playing cards.

By the time we arrived back at Kent station, we were quite merry. John Connolly, our pal, who was in charge of the

dining car and the bar, came up to our table and asked us if we would like another drink, as we would not be getting anymore.
All said yes, and you can bring us a double round. About 10 minutes later the train pulled into Cork and the train emptied.
We just sat at our table, and carried on with the card school, and drinking. About 20 minutes later, we heard this clunk, and the train started to move, but we took no notice.
The next thing it stops, and yes you've guessed it - we're all in Cobh, and it was now past midnight.
We just sat there, decided we would sleep on the train and return the following morning, which we did at no extra charge as we had not alighted from the train.
One Christmas Day morning I brought the lads in for training, this had never been heard of before, and they were expecting a hard session.
They were all sitting down in the dressing room. I said just sit there for five minutes, off I went into the Directors Room, broke the lock on the drinks cabinet, and walked back into the lads with plenty of the best beverages they could buy. You should have seen their faces, the hard training sessions turned into a hard-drinking session, and when we had finished off that lot, off we went to Tucker Allen's house, who was one of my players, and he only lived a few doors from the ground. More drink, more stories, and thank God, no training the next day.
It was around this time when some Council workers, were doing the pavements outside the ground, so I asked them if they could do me a favour and rip up the rotten floor in the dressing room, as rats and everything were running wild. They said 'yes' and they concreted the floor, good job it was too, it kept the walls up for another 15 years, and payment for this lovely job, a signed piece of paper from me admitting them into the ground 'free of charge' for all our home matches.

When the lads appeared for training the next day they thought they were in Wembley, but one of the players, Pat O'Mahony, noticed something was missing. Where's the Holy Water font gone, what was that?

It wasn't that old thing taped together with elastoplasts, that's the one he replied. "I am sorry mate, I threw it out. I thought it was a bird-bath.

St. Mary's legend the late Gerry Geaney pictured at home with Carl and John O'Neill on a visit back to Cork.

Philly Singleton, the man who kept soccer alive on the north side of Cork City and says the Dav was the greatest English player ever to kick a ball in Ireland. Also in the snap is one of the Dav's best mates John O'Neill from Derby.

*Carl pictured with his Cork Hibs team before a Eurpoean tie
against Valencia in Spain in 1971
Left to right; Joe O'Grady, Ray Cowhie, Wiggy, Frank Connolly and the Dav*

*Carl pictured with his Cork Hibs team before a Eurpoean tie in Spain
Left to right; Donie Wallace, the Dav, Austin Noonan, George O'Sullivan and Terry Young*

TALES OF CORK
Tea Pot Tunnel

I had not been in Cork very long when I was invited to the Sports Personality Award Dinner at the Imperial Hotel on the South Mall.

I went along with a lovely girl, Liz Moriarty, she had her own hairdressing salon and with us on the evening was my pal Jackie Morley and his wife, Joan. We arrived a bit late, anyway, this gentleman who was presenting the awards finally got to the last award and the dinner had come to an end.

We got up and walked down the large stairs into the foyer. I started talking to some people, when the gentleman who had been presenting the awards came over to me, and asked: "Dav could I have my photograph taken with you?" "Certainly," I replied, you have done a good job tonight Tea Pot." He laughed, I shouted to Jackie and the two girls to come over and have our photograph taken with the "Tea Pot." Yes, you probably guessed, it was that great man himself, the Prime Minister of Ireland, Jack Lynch.

The Taoiseach. He just laughed again. It was only later that I found out who he really was, what a lovely man and we remained friends until he died years later.

Every time I go through the Jack Lynch Tunnel, I think of him and that night, and smile.

CHARACTERS AROUND CORK

There was a lot of great characters around Cork at that time, a famous man in his own right, his name was 'Slobby Malone'. He would make his money off people looking for a parking spot. He would back you in, then come around to the driver's window, you would pay him what you like. No receipt or VAT ... magic.

I got to know Slobby very well, as on our match days he would always be doing his thing around the stadium. He called me Mr. Dav, always made me smile. He went one day to buy a trousers at the sale in Roches Stores. It was very busy, a lot of garments being sold. It was a trousers he wanted, he finds the pair he wanted, and puts them on the counter, the lady wraps them up and off he goes out of the store to the toilets on the quay.

He goes into the free one, taking his old trousers off, and puts the string around them in a parcel and throws them through the open window into the River Lee.

He then unwraps the brown parcel which he had put on top of the toilet, only to find that he had only picked up the wrong parcel in the shop. It was a shirt, that's my boy, but a lovely man. He was also very intelligent, but he did not let people know that side of him. He had a brother, and when their father died, he left one half of Patrick Street to 'Slobby' and the other half to his brother, then it was unequal wages. Ha ha.

CORK CELTIC 1967

All my time with Cork Celtic was fabulous, good players and great people who wanted to win, and listen. That was our secret for being successful. I trained them hard, brought in new training techniques, such as Parlov running. This was brought into the country from Sweden by a friend of mine Peter Keiling, a great miler and 1,500 metres runner. He ran against the great Derek Ibbitson, one of the first men to run a mile in under four minutes. Gordan Pirie was another, and he used to run at the Santry Stadium in Dublin with all the promotions in those days which were arranged by the great Billy Morton.

Peter's great race at that time was against Ireland's legendary Ronnie Delaney, Olympic Gold Medal winner in Melbourne in 1956, and one of the world's best at the time.

Our training consisted of sprinting more with the ball than ever before, pulse rates being checked to know if people were training properly, more tactics, and team meetings the day before matches and one extra day's training each week.

After our home games, I made sure everybody went to the same bar, for a drink and a chat about the game, and the lads could have an open discussion on things that happened during the game, this made them all talk collectively instead of just being individuals.

I played for the League of Ireland in 1968 at Windsor Park, Belfast and that was when the Troubles were bad in the North, so it was a bit scary.

My friend who played with me at Celtic, Pat O'Mahony, was also playing at left-back. He was a player ahead of his time, he would be known as a wing-back today, as he was an attacking player. We won 2-1 with yours truly getting the wining goal.

My next match for the League of Ireland team, was against the

Carl with Cork Celtic prior to a league game against Drums in 1967
Back: Donie Leahy, Tommy Taylor, Pat O'Mahony, John Carroll
Eamon Heffernan, John McCarthy, Front: Paddy Shortt, Charlie O'Mahony,
Carl Davenport, Dave O'Driscoll, Sidney Venner

English League at Barnsley. England had most of the World
Cup winning team on duty that night. Our strike force on that
night, was myself and my best pal, Dave Wigginton. Wiggy to
me and everybody then. We did everything together. We
lived together in digs at Mrs. Sheehan's in Douglas, we were
inseparable even in bed !

My best pal died about a decade ago, October 18, 2001, at the
young age of 51. It was like losing my brother.

Before the game, I got 50 to 60 telegrams that people had sent
from all over England wishing me well. That was nice. Then
a knock on the dressing room door, it was my old pal, Francis
Lee. He says I have just seen your name on the programme
and our other pal Mike Summerbee is also playing (we used to
be pals in Manchester) along with George Best, amazing.

The game itself went well, we only lost 3 – 0, and marking me
on that night was Paul Madeley and Norman Hunter, two of

the best players in the world at that time.

We went back to our hotel after the game, satisfied with our performance, and so was our manager, Liam Tuohy, who was a great winger with Shamrock Rovers and a lovely man.

At the hotel that night my pal John Whylie, who I played with at Preston North End and Stockport County, had brought along Alex Jefferies, who had broken his leg at the age of 22, but could have been one of the game's greatest players, but for that terrible injury.

In my career since becoming a pro, I scored over 300 goals but believe it or not I can only remember TWO of them.

Was I dreaming or was it me!

I lived life to the full, wine, women, and song - you name it, I did it. I would get £180 per week tax free, in 1969. Before the week was up, I had spent the lot, but, as you know you never think good things come to an end, but I did. People live their lives in very different ways, some people save up, others have big houses with big mortgages, they don't have a life, all the money goes into the house, which will still be there when they have gone to the local cemetery or the crematorium.

I thought differently and spent the cash on a good time - birds and booze - but that I could do because I trained hard and looked after myself.

THE BEST IRISH JOKE

Two Irishmen in England, Paddy from Cork and Sean from Kerry. They see this job advertised in the paper, it's for two people.

So they get an interview for the job, the receptionist greeted them, and tells them to take a seat, and that the boss will see them shortly. Paddy says to Sean, who was not that clever, when the boss asks me anything you always say one more than me, example, if I say 2, you say 3, Okay, fine says Sean.

Anyway the boss is ready to see them, they sit down in his office, the boss explains to them that the work is for two people, so that he was going to ask them some questions, but they both had to answer their individual questions correctly.

If they did, they would both get the job. First question to Paddy. What size of shoe are you, 8 was the reply. Sean 9, very good. Second question, Paddy, what waist are you, reply 32, Sean 33, very good.

Next what size collar are you Paddy, 15, 16 says Sean.

Excellent says the boss, if you both answer the next question, you have both got the job and can start on Monday. Great they say.

Last question then, Paddy what size hat are you 6/7/8 he replied. Quick as a flash, Sean says 9 – 10 – Jack.

Well I thought it was funny.

CORK HIBERNIANS

My time at Cork Hibernians was fantastic at the beginning, as the manager, Amby Fogarty bought me for a club record fee of £2,500, between two League of Ireland clubs. Amby was a good manager, a former Sunderland and Ireland international. His friend was Brian Clough, who was managing Derby County at the time, but went on to manage Nottingham Forrest to win the European Cup, not once but twice and that's how 'Wiggy' came to Cork.

Three other players - John Lawson, Sonny Sweeney and Tommy Henderson were brought over from Leeds United by myself and the late Jackie Lennox, who played for Cork United, and a good player he was too.

His son Brian was chairman of Cork City for a number of years.

Wiggy married Jackie's daughter, Francis, and the Lennox's had a chip shop chain, and I married Jean, whose family, the Crosbie's own Cork's two widely read newspapers - the *Irish Examiner* and the *Evening Echo.*

The story goes, that Wiggy used to wrap up his chips in Dav's paper.

Amby Fogarty was the man who made Cork Hibernians into the club it was, make no mistake about that. Who would have bought me from the opposition club Cork Celtic, and don't forget I was player-manager and successful, as we finished second in the League, but I was the League's top scorer too. Amby was putting the great Hibs team together. Ray Cowhie and Charlie O'Mahony also came to Hibs as well, on my recommendation.

I remember us playing Dundalk, it was Ray Cowhie's first game for us. Before the game, all our shirts were hung on these pegs, I decided to get ready for the game early. After about

Carl on a visit to The Lord Mayor's Office at City Hall in Cork in 2008 in the company of Donal O'Flynn (centre) and ex-Cork City boss Pat Dolan.

The victorious Cork Hibernians team, unbeaten in the league (1970/71)
pictured before the local derby with Cork Celtic at Turners Cross
Back Row left to right; John Lawson, Sonny Sweeney, Noel O'Mahony, Joe O'Grady
Frank Connolly, John Herrick. Front Row left to right; Gerry Finnigan, Miah Dennehy,
Carl Davenport, Dave Bacuzzi, Dave Wigginton, Donie Wallace

five minutes in walks Amby, "What are you doing Dav?" he said. "Getting ready for the game," I replied. "Who said you are playing? Get changed back." Five minutes later, he announces the team, and "Dav you can get ready to play now," he said. That was just to show the rest that he was Boss, he was spot on.

He was always making an example of me, then he would say to me later, laughing, 'You know I only do it to keep the rest of them on their toes.'

A great man that Amby. He left the club later under very strange goings on with the directors, who interfered with team selection. Nothing new there.

Austin Noonan took over from Amby, a nice man, had been a great player in his day along with a great friend of mine, Donie Leahy, who was Austin's striking partner.

Austin did a great job as manager, along with Georgie O'Sullivan, a class act together, and we were now winning everything in sight, but the directors wanted a big name in charge from England.

First to come over was Bobby Collins, a great player in his day with Leeds United and Scotland. It was my job to take him out, entertain him that was my best job ever. His favourite tipple was Rye and Dry. We had some great nights mostly in the Intercontinental, the old Jury's hotel on the Western Road.

He was only a small dapper man, but he knew his football, he had been there and done it. I really wanted him to take the job, but he decided it was not for him, and he took the Morton job back home in Scotland. But why did the directors want another manager? They had a good one in Austin, why upset the team. It would have won the League for the next five years. It was the best and there will never be one like it again. You better believe that, it will always be the greatest team ever to play in the League of Ireland. It had everything.

After 12 months they got a man called Dave Bacuzzi, from England. They might as well have got Mickey Mouse ! As anybody could have managed that team and won.

To start off, he dropped Frankie Connolly, a winger in his early days, but was moulded into an excellent right full-back, skilful and passed a good ball, but he had to go, it was Dave Buccuzi's position. That was the start of it. He did not like me as I stole all of the glamour and headlines, how sad is that.

He would give me extra training, more than the rest of the team. He made my life hell, he tried to break me, but he had no chance of that, I was too strong a character.

Waterford wanted me, and Glentoran up north but John Crowley, director, increased my wages to £180 per week, not bad for 1971.

The manager didn't like this either, as I was on more money than him. When I did leave a couple of years later, Cork Hibernians went into liquidation and I still blame that man for his part in Cork Hibernians decline.

Amby Fogarty / Austin Noonan's Team
Joe O'Grady
Frank Connolly Martin Sheehan Noel O'Mahony John Herrick
John Lawson   Sonny Sweeney
Miah Dennehy Carl Davenport Dave Wiggingtoon Terry Young

Other Players: John Brohan, Donie Wallace and Jerry Finnegan.

I had just won the League with Cork Hibernians, their first League Championship in 1970, plus the honour of doing that. We got invited to Spain to play two friendly matches in the close season.

So off we went, a party of about thirty-five people, to a holiday resort called Loret de Mar, they also had a football team, and the ground was only 200 yards from our hotel, which was great.

Our first game was not for four days. On the first day there I met this beautiful German girl on the beach, and she was staying in the hotel, overlooking the football ground.

Her balcony was about seven floors up. I got involved with the lovely Helga, and I had gone missing from our hotel for two days and had also missed training.

On the second night of training, around 6pm, the lads were on the pitch, and Donie Wallace, one of our players spotted me on the balcony, seven floors up.

I had a bottle of champagne and was smoking a large cigar, with a fantastic, topless blond.

Training stopped and they all gave me a rousing ovation. Scored again!

When the night of the match came, half-way through the game, the floodlights failed for about 15 minutes. I still think it was Helga re-charging her vibrator !

EARLY DAYS ON LEESIDE

In January, 1967 I arrived in Cork by car and was met at the Metropole Hotel on MacCurtain Street by the three directors, Richie Neville, John Horgan and Paddy Barry of Cork City.

These were three tough cattle dealers. Also with them was the great man himself, Donie Forde, the club secretary. We chatted, and then Ray Cowhie and Donal Leahy arrived.

Two great players of their time, but more importantly, two great guys. After the meeting the two lads said, do you like a drink and would you like one. Yes, I replied, but this was Saturday night, and we were playing on Sunday in the local derby down the 'Lodge.

So it was goodbye to the directors, who thought I was going back to my new digs down the Mardyke. I don't think so, my new team mates took me down to a little back street pub in Merchant's Street, called McAuliffe's.

As we entered, they pushed me into a little snug, with curtains around it, so nobody, only the barman could see who was there. That was my first introduction to the magical city of Cork.

We played the next day and I got the winning goal, a dream start. That night I think I finished up in the Arcadia and the rest is history, as they say.

At this time both Celtic and Hibernians were bottom of the league, crowds of 300 were watching us, and I ended up scoring 15 goals in 13 games between January and April.

The following season, 1968-1969 I was made payer manager at 23, the youngest in the history of the game, at a professional level in Ireland.

We finished second in the League that year and crowds of 18,000 people watching every home game, what a turn around from the season before.

My players were fantastic professionals. I gave two young lads, I signed, their debuts, Paddy Shortt and John Carroll, and they did not let me down. They also mixed in well with the established players like Ray Cowhie, Pat O'Mahony, Donie Leahy, Charlie O'Mahony, Frank McCarthy and Tony 'Tucker' Allen. These were all big names, but age was catching up on them. But with the right training and belief in me, they were fantastic and I will always be thankful to them. I also had Jackie Morley training with us, he was playing with bitter rivals, Waterford, at the time, but it was easier to train with us, as he lived in Cork.

Jackie will tell you we trained hard, but it was enjoyable, and I think it put a few more years on to his career. He was by far the best centre-half in the League of Ireland, and I can tell you that with authority, as I played against him, and have the stitches to prove it.

My life in Cork was active to say the least, even Kathy Barry's was full most nights.

The brother of Charlie O'Mahony, Mick, changed the words of a Johnny McEvoy song, *Whiskey on a Sunday*, to Drinking and Women all the Week and Four Goals on a Sunday, the reason was we had just beaten St. Patrick's Athletic, 6 – 1 and I scored four.

I met one of the loves of my life around this period, she was called Katherine, a beautician. I chased her around the city for six months, she had a mini Cooper. I was in the Sunbeam Rapier, it was red, and I had just bought it brand new from a showroom in Bolton, when I'd gone home on holiday. I was with my pal Steve Fagan, and we went into the showroom. I knew the salesman, he was known as one-eyed Alf, yes, he only had one eye. How much is it I asked, £1,500 his replay. I explained to him that I was taking it out of the country to Ireland. He tells me, as long as you take it out of the UK, you don't have to pay tax on it, and I can let you have the car for £1,000. Fantastic I will have it. One year later in Cork, I found out it was not legal what I'd done. I could never get road tax on it, so I used a Guinness label. But what a car it was, in those days people called it the Hoover, as it picked up all the bits of fluff around the town.

I finally did get to meet Katherine, and went out with her for a few years, and then it turned horribly wrong. She told me we should have a break for six months, as I was messing about, and not being fair to her, and that if I changed my ways, we would get back together and that would be it. In the meantime, I had met Jean who was to become my wife, and I was in love. We got married in secret in Bolton. Nobody knew, even my landlady Mrs. Sheehan, did not know and she was good friends with Katherine.

We had the wedding and the day after, had to fly back to Dublin on Sunday, as I was playing a match for Cork Hibernians at Dalymount Park.

We got off the plane and into the airport, and there it was on all the Sunday papers, front page, the Dav marries newspaper magnate's daughter, George Crosbie was one of the owners of the 'Cork Examiner,' can you imagine the stick I got off the team, but not as much as I got when I arrived back in Cork.

When I lived in Cork, I had two fantastic landladies. When I arrived I was in with a wonderful family, the Hartnett's. Mrs Hartnett, her husband Dan and son Neill. Mrs. Hartnett was a niece of Richie Neville, the cattle dealer and director of Cork Celtic. The address of my digs was No. 1, Maryville, Mardyke

Walk, across the road from the Cork County Cricket Ground, where I used to play in the Cork Leagues. I did win a league medal with them and I wasn't a bad cricketer.

In the digs, there were six students staying there, as well as myself, a lad called John Doyle, who was a good pal, who was one educated son of a bitch. I heard he went on to be one of the top men in his profession. When I moved to Cork Hibernians, I changed digs and went to St. Cecilia's, Douglas Lawn to stay with Mrs. Sheehan, her husband Larry and children Marion, Dan, Claire and Jo, a fantastic family.

On the first meeting, I knocked on the door, Wiggy was with me, he was carrying the cases, as we both moved in. It was £5 each full board, washing and ironing done as well for that. I think I will move back. I still go to see Mrs. Sheehan when I am over, Larry passed away, a few years ago. He would come to all the Hibs home matches, and would bring Dan along. John Lawson and Tommy Henderson also moved in with us after that, two Scotsmen, they tried to get the two of them in at £5 for the two. They were great times, and when I visit, I sit down with Mrs. Sheehan and reminisce about bygone days, over one of her special cups of Barry's tea.

Carl in a packed Swan & Cygnet pub as Cork Hibernians celebrate an FAI Cup
triumph...... happy days indeed. Check out the faces .... Jim Clancy (RIP) behind
the bar, Waterford's Jackie Morley (with son Pat in his arms),
referee Bobby Duggan and Joe Horgan.

Cork Hibernians Club Secretary and part owner John Crowley (RIP) pictured with
his wife Louise and Dave Wigginton and his then wife Frances Lennox
at the club's annual dinner in the early 70's

NIGHTLIFE

One of the first licensed clubs was the Carousel, open from 9pm to, I can't remember?

Music, dancing and another sport, I just can't think what it was, a field event in the Olympic Games. Great music that time in the early 70s, Lola was a big hit at that time, by the Kinks, and in later years, Ray Davies, the lead singer, became my brother-in-law, by marriage, not through sleeping with him.

Somebody once asked me which was the best club I played for? I replied the Carousel.

Wiggy and myself would go out of town for a drink, where we thought nobody would recognise us. This particular day we went out towards Ovens, just outside Cork City. I used to say hottest place in Ireland, we find this little old pub, after a couple of pints, Wiggy went to the toilet, which was outside, 50 yards away. When he came back he said to the landlord, that there was no lock on the toilet door, the landlord's reply was, "I have never had a bucket of shite stolen in the past 50 years I've been here". Then he added, "Neither did my father before me."

In those days, I only drank halves, to make it look good if anybody saw me out. One day the directors of Cork Hibernians had me in front of them, they said I had been seen drinking in Cobh, which I had, but the same night I had been in Blarney, Kinsale and Crosshaven.

I said I could not have drunk much in Cobh, as I have witnesses to say I was also in the other places. They gave me a pay rise, as I must have been spending a fortune on petrol.

The man who kept Cork Hibernians going was John Crowley, a great man. He was to Hibs, what Donie Forde was to Celtic. Great footballing ambassadors to their respective clubs and to

75

Cork itself. At Cork Hibs I was on £180 per week, tax free, paid on Sunday, broke on the following Friday, had to get a sub off him. When you're young, you do daft things, but I had made my mind up, I was going to enjoy every minute, it's no good having a lot of money when you are old, and can't do the things you want. So that's what I did, and I knew by the time I would be 40 that I could be sleeping on a park bench - I made the choice.

TENNIS

I played tennis every year in the Rushbrooke tournament down in Cobh, a beautiful spot, all grass courts then in 1969. I played with Kieran Madden, a good Squash player and a good friend of mine.

I also played with my then brother-in-law, Jim Good of Kinsale, we were married to Jean and Anne Crosbie, of the Cork Examiner group. We have since parted.

I used to play in England, my auntie taught me to play from the age of five. When I came to Cork, I started to play with Jim in Bandon at the local Grammar School, we were both fit men.

Jim being a hockey and rugby player. We had some great battles down there. We played a match in the Sunday's Well tournament, and over 100 people watched me and Jim play Declan Fitzgerald and Sean Hehir. I think we lost 6-4, 4-6, 6-4 in an amazing game.

One of my favourite tennis clubs is Argideen Vale, down in Timoleague, I used to call it 'TOP OF THE LEAGUE,' because at soccer that's where we always were.

The tennis club is situated in the middle of a forest. Six fantastic grass courts, in fact it's the only one left, to still have all grass courts.

The club also ran croquet. A gentleman dressed in stripped blazer, tie and flannels, rings an old bell and everyone enjoys afternoon tea - fantastic. On the way back after tennis, we would come back along the coast road, looking over the estuary to Courtmacsherry. Sometimes, we would have a swim and go into the Pink Elephant, a beautiful pub/restaurant owned by a good old friend of mine, Bill Wafer and we'd have a laugh and a few pints before returning to Kinsale, where I was living at the time.

As you know, Kinsale is one of the oldest and most established towns in Ireland.

I had a very good friend in Kinsale, his name was John Light, a deep sea diver, who had secured the rights from Lloyds Insurance, London, to own the famous ship, the Lusitania.

John was a former US Navy diver and came to Ireland in the early 1960's with three or four others of his trade to dive on the Lusitania, the Cunard liner sunk on May 7, 1915 - ten miles off the Old Head of Kinsale after being hit by the German submarine U20 during World War One.

Johh was a very popular man around town and while here met and married Muriel Acton of the local hotel, farming and hardware business.

He came and went from Kinsale on a number of trips and visited England on business regarding the wreck.

He seemed happy and the two were a fashionable part of the local scene.

There was always a bit of mystery about John and the dives he made on the sunken liner where more than 1,200 lives had been lost.

There was also a good deal of criticism of the British Admiralty and their handling of the whole affair.

There were a good number of rumours floating about the

77

purpose of his dives, the least of which was not the purported treasures she carried down with her when she sunk.

He was hired by the BBC to help make a film on the ship and he gained a good deal of notoriety in Ireland, England and the USA as a result of the dives.

Something happened during this period to change John and he became less out-going, whether it was from the dives or the public attention he attracted, no one was able to discern.

DUBLIN AND COMING TO THE END

Football is a strange occupation, when you're young you have no fears about making mistakes, going into tackles for 50-50 balls, going up in the air with a big ugly centre-half.

But as you get older, say 28, you know too much about the game and start watching out for yourself. I did have everything, two good feet and won everything in the air, that was because I had been coached, alongside the great Nat Lofthouse, who was the best ever header of a ball, since time began.

It's all about timing, jumping up there, and staying there, head comes back, then forward and your head connects with the ball, sounds easy, try it!

Just lost my drift there for a while, but I was visually going through the action, getting back to the point of knowing too much about the game, it then goes the other way.

I was a fearless man when I went onto the pitch, also wanted every ball, in team talks when I was player manager, I would say, play every ball you can to me, if you don't you won't get a game next week. Ha Ha!

In later years, I was playing out my career at St. Patrick's Athletic, Jack Burkett, was manager, he played with Nottingham Forest, a lovely man, I would go from Cork on the train to Dublin, stay at the Green Isle Hotel. I would make arrangements to see this beautiful girl every time I stayed there, she would drive out from the city and meet me. This was great until I rang Jack up the night before the game, and said I was ill and could not play the following day. He said he was very sorry and hoped I would get well soon.

Champagne, steaks ordered to my room, fantastic, all on expenses, and ready for action.

Knock on the door, more champagne, no Jack Burkett and a director, what could I say, you might as well come in and have a drink, I said.

This girl, half naked, in the room, and I just got away with a fine. I had to pay for the two bottles of champagne. Continuing my story, after one match, half-way through the season, a friend of mine, Vinny McGuire who was in the team at St. Pat's previously, he played with the great Waterford side which, also had another great player in Jackie Morley, the best I had ever played against in Ireland.

I remember playing in a top of the league clash at Waterford for Cork Hibernians, it was St. Patrick's Day, very appropriate, it was pissing rain, big crowd, 15,000, I went up for this ball with Jackie, clash of heads, I knew it was bad, a big gash on the back of my head, blood everywhere.

On comes our trainer, old Georgie Sullivan, quite deaf, but a lovely, lovely man. He gets out his bag and magic sponge, I am semi-conscious in the mud, so George looks at it and puts a load of Vaseline into the gash.

On comes the ambulance man, he says to Georgie, what have you put Vaseline in the wound for, he says, to keep the rain out. I was taken to hospital and needed six stitches.

To finish this chapter off, Vinny Maguire after one particular match for St. Patrick's Athletic, he says to me, you are not the player you were, why I asked? Because you used to frighten us all with your strength, knocking people about, yes, he was right, I was older and wiser, but is does not work in later years, you grow less fearless, you know the pitfalls, that's when you are coming to the end of your magic life in football, and it will never be the same again. Age has caught up with you, and you are the last to know.

BEYOND THE LEE

The reason I left Cork was that my father had been diagnosed with cancer.

I got a telephone call from my aunt in Bolton telling me that my Dad was in hospital. I lived in Douglas with my then wife Jean and my two children Mark aged 5, and Jason aged 4.

I got the first plane out of Cork to Manchester leaving my family at home. I was met by my aunt, and she told me my Dad did not want me to worry, typical of him.

We got to the hospital, Dad was pleased to see me. I went to see the specialist who was going to do the operation. I asked "What were his chances?" he said, "very good." I then said, "Well carry on." My wife Jean and the two children came over, our house put up for sale, and sold immediately.

In the mean time, Dad was still in hospital, had the operation. I went to see the doctor at the hospital, and he told me that my Dad had six months to live.

I was shocked and upset. I went to my dad's bed. He said he felt good, after the operation, he thought it had been successful, so I went along with that. We all went on holiday together to Torquay as my mother had passed away a few years earlier.

It was a fabulous holiday, Wife, kids and myself and my dad.

But I knew he had only months to live.

Time went by and I signed for Lancaster, in the Northern Premier League. I had not kicked a ball for five years, but had kept myself reasonably fit, as I always trained on my own, three days a week, even to this day.

I came home one night after a game and Dad had an idea he was dying and said, "That hospital has killed me!" We watched *Match of the Day* together, kids in bed, just Dad, myself and Jean, who was only 21, and Dad passed away in my arms on the settee.

Jean telephoned the doctor, and I talked to my Dad, and told him how much I loved him, everything he had done for me all my life, and to this day, I still think he heard me. I felt better for telling him. He was a magic dad, I still go down to the grave and talk to him. He always told me that when he died, he did not want a stone on him, as if he had any chance of getting out of there, he didn't want any weight on him, so he has only got a headstone.

My wife Jean had never seen anyone die before, so it was very distressing. A week or so after the funeral on November 20, I said to Jean why don't you take the lads back to Cork for a couple of weeks before Christmas, and when you come back I will have all the presents, bikes, toys, etc sorted.

After a couple of weeks of no contact, I got a telephone call from a solicitor for their family, saying that my wife and children were not returning to me and that she wanted a divorce. I was shocked, upset and, more to the point, I had lost everybody I loved - my Dad and my family in the space of three weeks. It nearly destroyed me, needless to say, it was the worst Christmas I have ever had in my life and I don't like Christmas to this day. I wonder why?

When I arrived back to Bolton after my time in Ireland, my

pals were all still around Bally, Francis Lee, Freddie Hill all ex-Bolton Wanderers and England. One of Fred's pals was a young lad, who had heard all about me from friends of mine.

It was Tony Knowles, yes, the snooker player. I met him at a party and could not get away from him, in fact I went around to his house in Bolton for my tea, and lived there for the next five years.

During that time he had gone up the World Ranking system and reached No. 2 beating Steve Davis 10-1 at the Crucible in Sheffield. His house in Bolton was an old school house which he had converted into a beautiful place with a snooker table that had been used for a World Snooker Final. He and his mother, father and two brothers before that lived and ran a Conservative Club just outside Bolton.

Tony, as a boy, used to play all the regulars, on a snooker table that they had in the club and that was how he got to be so good at the game.

By the time he was 16 he was beating everybody in Bolton, and went on to reach No. 2 in the World. If you are No. 2 in this Big World, you are not just good, but great.

He would give me 70 start and beat me most times. I was not bad, having played a bit as a boy, but I improved my game with Tony, on how to play safe. If you left him one red, he would clear up.

He also had a beautiful house on Lake Windermere, on the lake itself. There are only 12 houses with lake frontage. On going down from the house, fantastic gardens, at the bottom two grass tennis courts, where we played everyday, and 15 yards on was the lake, jetty and a boathouse and his Mastercraft Speedboat which he used for water-skiing.

We went out in the boat one day, he gets the skies and I steer the boat. He said keep away from the passenger launch, when it comes.

I had forgotten about me towing Tony. The wash off this big boat nearly drowned him, I looked back and all I could see was this small head in the water, about 600 yards back, anyway I picked him up, eventually.

He loved doing anything but practice snooker. I would say let's get on the table, he had one in the Lake House. I will do a bit of gardening, loved gardening, should have been called Tony Thrower. One day we walked down to the tennis court. He started messing about with a football, I said give it to me. I started juggling with the ball, keeping it up, one foot then the other foot, to both knees to both shoulders, on my head and back down, shoulders, knees and feet.

He was amazed at this, and he wanted to be able to do this more than anything. World Championship, four birds in one bed, to beat me, that's all he wanted, tried for an hour, nowhere near me, but he's still No. 2 in the World.

About 12 months later, I am up at the house with him, he says, shall we have a walk down the garden, OK, I said. When we get down the garden, I see the football still around, watch this he says. Well he did the trick, I could not believe it, but what he had done everyday was to practice with this ball, never picked up a cue to practice his snooker. The moral of this story is, practice makes perfect – on the other side of the coin, he was No. 2, in 12 months he dropped to No. 8, and which one made the most, money, he's still trying to work that one out.

STORIES

Francis Lee, also trained race horses, years after he had finished playing, plus making a living out of paper kitchen towels and toilet rolls. In fact a multi-millionaire, thanks most likely as the saying comes from: 'Where there's muck, there's brass.

'One day at Haddock Park Racecourse, he had a runner in the 3pm race. So he was there in the morning with the horse. He was giving the horse something out of the palm of his hand, and who comes along, only Lord Leverhulme, the Local Steward of the course.

He asked Francis what he was giving the horse, he replied a lump of sugar. "My Lord, would you like one," so he said "Yes," as he thought it could be an illegal substance.

The time of the race comes round, and Francis is giving his jockey his final instructions, of how he has planned the race, "Take your time coming out of the starting stalls, keep her just behind the leaders, two furlongs out, let her go, and don't worry if anything passes you, it will only be Lord Leverhulme!"

RACING AT CHELTENHAM

I used to go the Cheltenham Festival every March, to see the best jumpers in the world. I had already rode most of them !

On the first day of the meeting, Tuesday, with my friend and racing pal, Michael Gildea, we left our hotel in my gold Jaguar car. Suits on, Crombie overcoats and Trilbys We arrive through the main entrance, go one hundred yards and out jumps an official, "STOP!"

But let me enlighten you first, there was an old race horse trainer called Neville Crump, famous, for training Grand National winners, who I had met many times in the past, especially at Middleham in Yorkshire, where he trained, but he had a horse running in the 3.05pm that afternoon. It was called Richdee. So here I am confronted by this official, I wound my car window down, I was smoking a big cigar, I said, "Excuse me sir, I am Sir Llewellyn Davenport Crump, and I have a runner in the 3.05pm race," in a very posh voice. He said, "Would you please park over there in the Owners car park, Sir," and then he saluted us both.

For the next two days of racing, we just drove in, he saluted us, and we parked the car, in the best spot, and we were handed a race card.

I enjoyed being Sir Llewellyn Davenport Crump, where the name came from I don't know, it just came out of my mouth.

Actually it was at the same meeting that my pal John Horgan who was a director of Cork Celtic Football Club, had a runner. I met him in the Golden Valley. He was with Mouse Morris and Richard Hannon, two great racehorse trainers, but in those days Mouse Morris was a jockey riding John's horse the following day.

John said it had a chance and it readily won coming over the last hurdle and on the stands rail winning by two lengths. The horse was called Northern Game.

One year I went to the festival with Bally, we had a few drinks, within minutes Mick Channon and Steve Smith Eccles, a good jump jockey, myself and Alan then went to a party at David Nicholson's (trainer) daughter's house, what a night and morning. There were five jockeys there, and believe it or not they rode the first five horses home in the Gold Cup, all trained by Michael Dickenson, and that feat will never be done ever again, it's history.

Who said drink never wins?

Well 12 months later at the Cheltenham meeting, an Irish horse won the Champion Hurdle, it was called 'For Auction' owned by the Cunningham's and the owners, if I'm not mistaken, owned Shamrock Rovers.

I was staying in a hotel-pub style place with a huge car park at the back of it. So we set off for the track, myself and Mike Gildea.

Did the Llewellyn Crump bit again, and was on to the track. It was a good day. After racing we headed for the famous Golden Valley Hotel, a fine place, it was actually used to film the famous soap, *Crossroads*.

You will remember it if you are my age. My pal John Horgan was there, also the surgeon who operated on my knee and removed my cartilage, Surgeon St. John Connell, who was then John's father-in-law.

The time was now about 9pm, a guy comes up to us, and says are you with the Horgan party. I said yes. Go into that big room over there, do you like champagne, he said, well go and drink as much as you can.

We have won the Champion Hurdle with For Auction, and had backed it anti post at 80/1. I knew a lot of the people in there, as it was an Irish winner. The two owners then realised there was no piano, they only went out and bought one from the local music shop, and had to get this guy to open up the shop.

A fantastic night was had by all, then came reality. I had to drive back to our hotel, which was a couple of miles away. Could I find the pub where we were staying, and also I did not know the name of it. How stupid is that. I even asked a policeman, if he knew a pub with a big car park. I was desperate now, tired and wanted my bed, that's unusual!

We did find the place, but it was 3.30am. by this time. We wake up in the morning, look out the window, the car park is as big as a football ground.

GEORGE O'SULLIVAN AND VALENCIA

WE played Valencia in one of the European Cup games, the manager at that time was one of the greatest centre-forwards of all-time and his name was Alfredo di Stefano.

He played for Real Madrid along with the great Hungarian footballer Puskas, Hiddiguti, Santa Maria, Gento and company - they won the European Cup six times - no mean feat that.

Well our second round clash was about to kick-off and we had Austin Noonan, the assistant manager and Georgie O'Sullivan in the dug-out reading the menu for the after-match dinner.

In the opposition dug-out which was only a few yards away, we had di Stefano and the top European coach at the time - a man called Rocco who could speak a little English.

The whistle goes for the start of the game and after about 10 minutes John Lawson, our Scottish-born midfielder, goes down injured.

He's lying there on the park and no sign of George who had a bit of a hearing problem.

The two lads are still looking at the menu in our dug-out.

So Rocco in his broken English shouts across to our dug-out and says: "Georgie, Georgie sponge."

George replied: "Oh yes, and custard."

That's one of the many yarns on a foreign trip that has gone down in Cork soccer folklore.

At Cheltenham, I would meet a lot of people from Cork, Jimmy Edwards and his wife Paula who have a lovely pub-restaurant in Kinsale, the gourmet capital of the world, never mind Ireland and the UK.

One of my sons and their son were born on the same day in adjacent beds in hospital.

Also at the meeting with me were good friends Pat and Celine O'Donnell, who own the Finder's Inn in Nohoval, Co. Cork.

In fact, I sold them a race horse from a friend of mine, John Burgess in Bolton and he owed a large stable at Middleham in north Yorkshire.The then trainer of the horse was David Moorehead and they had close on 80 horses in training.

Celine was anxious to buy this particular horse called 'Taberna Lord' so I did the deal on her behalf and the horse went on to win a lot of hurdle races, one at Haydock Park, the Swinton Handicap and the other big race at Cheltenham, the Coral Handicap Hurdle.

Yes, it was that good a horse.

GEORGE BEST

I am writing this, and the best player the world has ever seen, George Best, has just passed away, a legend!

I knew him from the early 60s. I played against him many times for Bolton 'A' team with my life-long friend Alan Ball. I got a hat-trick one day against Manchester United 'A' at the Cliff. That was United's training ground. I had forgotten about the goals I scored that day until Alan, informed me only five years ago. I must be going senile, but I do remember the three of us going out on Saturday night, many times together. I wonder why I remember that. The next time I met him, after that, was when I was playing with Cork Hibernians, we played two pre-season friendlies in England, one was against Dunstable Town, a millionaire owned the club, and George was playing for them. He arrived in a white Rolls Royce, was late, and kick-off was put back half an hour, to accommodate him. Things don't change.

The last time we met up, was in Dubai, of all places, in 1986. I was with Tony Knowles, the snooker player, he was playing in a tournament over there. It was sponsored by Sheik Abdulla, on behalf of the Arab Emirates.

We stayed in this fantastic hotel and were treated like royalty. An exhibition match was arranged for the Abdulla Family in the main lounge, half the size of a football field. The table was in the middle, and around the wall areas, were tables of every food you could imagine and enough champagne to sink the Titanic.

Tony was playing the famous Alex 'Hurricane' Higgins, just three frames, then who walks in the main entrance – George. We had not seen each other for 10 years. It surprised us both. John Parrott's manager, took photographs of us both, and later sent me the photograph. I am looking at it this minute as it hangs on the wall in my lounge, where I am writing this, and it's brought a few tears to my eyes.

Well as the night progressed, and a lot of stories were told about the past, the laughter, the situations we had both been in and believe me, George and myself had a lot in common, things had gone very much the same pattern through our lives, and we both did not regret one moment.

As I said before, you choose the way you want to live, and if you are happy with that, it's nobody else's business, only your own. So by the time we had finished our night or should I say early morning, you know the champagne I mentioned earlier on, we had made a hell of a hole in it, to the tune that there wasn't much left.

Just to say a few words about George on this sad day, he was a genius with a football, one that the world will never see again. You better believe that. He was also a lovely lad and a gentleman, and he will be remembered as one of the greatest footballers of all time.

Goodbye, George, thanks for the memories, you were special.

JOHNNY BURROWS

A friend of mine from Bolton, Johnny Burrows, he's also a friend of Bally's. He worked as a right hand man for Brian Buckley a self made millionaire, through Carpet Manufacturing. Well they went into London to a push club to meet some friends, Denis Law and George Best and Paddy Crerand at 7pm. They sat at the best table, the Bunny Girl type waitress came over for the order. So John says, three bottles of pink champagne, off she went and returned back with the order, (ice buckers etc.). The waitress says to John, I am from Cork and I know somebody who speaks like you.

As quick as a flash he says I can tell you who you are thinking about, you can't she replied, he then says I am a mind reader and I am at the London Palladium all week and I will tell you now. He started rubbing his head and groaning and said there is a D and a port, my head is hurting just a second the name's Davenport. She can't believe it, she then calls her sister over who was also working there, tells her what had happened and John says quickly: "And he's fucked you as well, and she replied he has, he has.
Very clever, as he knew there was only one person in Cork who has the same accent as himself, me.

Sporting worlds collide in Dubai of all places!
The Dav who was on tour with then snooker World No. 2 Tony Knowles from Bolton
meets up with the legendary George Best. Bestie is the one with the beard!

Carl and Dave Wigginton enjoy a quiet pint on a day off in Bandon, Co. Cork
just a few months before 'Wiggie' died..

DARK DEEDS IN KILLARNEY

In 2004, myself and Alan (Ball) went across to Cork, at the invitation of Peter O'Regan, a good friend of mine, who was also a director of Cork City, years ago. We stayed at Blarney, and Peter had arranged a Charity Golf Day for us.

This was a great trip for Alan, as his lovely wife, Leslie, had died of cancer, after a long battle, a few weeks before.

Playing with me that day was Mick Fitzgerald, a famous jump jockey, who also rode for the Queen (I rode for myself), and a lovely guy, who liked a good laugh.

After we had finished playing, we had a meal in the club house, and a cabaret, but to my surprise, an old friend was performing, and I had not seen him for 30 years, and that was in the Opera House, in that famous Cork show *the Swans*, in which he and Paddy Comerford took the mick out of me, saying it must be him, the Carousal has just closed, and that's 'the Dav' who has just gone past in his car,

Yes, it was the great Billa O'Connell, the top comedian of his time, what a fantastic night we had, I will always remember that day, perfect, and met many past sportsmen of my time, they told many stories, which are always good ones, not like some of mine.

Well it did Alan the world of good, and took his mind off the loss of his wife and helped him to get his life back on track. The next day off we went to Killarney Week, to the races, which were on and Alan had been a regular visitor in the past, and had booked us into an hotel he knew well and typically we got the best rooms.

In the morning we had breakfast, with a few friends who were over from England, who knew Alan well, got the racing paper, did some studying, and off we went to the races.

At the track, I bumped into a legend of Gaelic Football, of

years ago, in my own days. I said to him "Are you Mick O'Connell", he replied: "Yes I am," I said to him, "You were my hero." "What's your name," he said, "Carl Davenport," I replied, "You were my hero too, amazing!"

He used to come and watch me play at Flower Lodge, but in a flat cap, to disguise himself. It was not permitted for Gaelic footballers to go and watch soccer in those days because of that ridiculous ban.

We returned to the hotel after the race meeting and had a meal, and eight of us go into the lounge for a few drinks. It was about 11pm by now, and not very busy, as most residents had retired, as another day's racing was on the agenda for tomorrow.

So chatting among ourselves, one of the party said that BA was at the bar, he being a top jump jockey, me being a race horse man, I went over, he was with a big guy. I shook him by the hand, best of luck tomorrow, as he was riding again the next day.

I went back to my company and as the night went on, people went to bed, at different intervals. Alan went about 3.15am, leaving me and a pal of his to have our last drinks.

He then left, said goodnight and into the lift. I was just ready for going, B.A.G and his minder, walk down between the tables and chairs, and he says let's have him. I stand up quick and the big guy, Gorilla, throws a punch, so I defend myself. After a couple of exchanges, I fell to the floor in between some tables and chairs.

They then started kicking me while I lay on the floor. Blood everywhere, I tell them I have had two heart attacks in the past 12 months, they took no notice. Just then the lift door opens and a man, who had to be up early because he was driving to Dublin, told them to stop, or that they would kill me.

He took me up to our room, where Alan was asleep, my face smashed up, blood everywhere, what a mess, but I was just happy that I was still alive, thanks to my anonymous life saver. I have thanked him since as I do believe I owe him my life.

The day after the doctor saw me, and said I was very lucky my heart had stood up to it. This particular doctor knew me as he graduated from University College Cork, and was a regular supporter when I played for Cork Hibernians.

He only knew me by name as I was unrecognisable. He was also the Race course doctor. Apparently the two attackers have more form than the horses, not nice people. It was all covered up by the Gardaí and the hotel proprietors. This type of local publicity was not good publicity and the whole bloody episode was kept under wraps - till now. As for BA he just thought I was an English tourist and where he comes from they are not liked.

My friends from 96FM helped me a lot. Frank O'Brien who was in Tenerife at the time, rang the hotel and asked what was going on, as they just wanted to keep it quiet.

I was up in my room for two days without food or drink. They just wanted me out of the way. I was in a very bad way, so my great friend Neil Prenderville, arrives down from Cork, and took me back to his house in Douglas. God I was glad to see him, and cannot thank him enough. This was the worst three days of my life in Killarney, a good name for it KILL. But what kind of human beings would do that to a 61 year old man, only cowards and low life people. I will never forget that night and the two bastards who did that cowardly deed.

BALLY DIES

When my best friend Alan Ball died, it was a big shock to me. He was only 61.

I was in Spain at the time, but Alan's son, Jimmy was in contact with me.

I returned for the funeral at Winchester Cathedral. All the World Cup team of 1966 were present. Also at the funeral were Alex Ferguson (now Sir Alex), my pals, relations from Bolton, Mike Summerbee, Francis Lee as well as many other famous people. Of course, the TV cameras were there in force. After the funeral a reception was held at Southampton Football Club, who had been kind enough to offer their facilities. I had been speaking with Mick Channon, ex-footballer who by now was one of the biggest racehorse trainers in England. I had been told that a certain horse would go close in the 7.40pm at Chepstow, by this time, I'd had a few drinks of course, but having an account with William Hill, I rang in a bet. £500 on a horse called Katie Boo. I told my pals what I had done, they could not believe it, and neither could I - £500 quid on a nag.

By this time people were leaving in dribs and drabs, so I was staying at Alan's house and I suggested that we should go to Alan's local "The Jolly Farmer" in Wardash, owned by a lovely Irishman by the name of Pat Martin.

We left the local at 4am and off to Bally's house, and into bed. In the morning, I went into his beautiful garden. Stood where he had died, putting the fire out, which had started on the compost heap after he'd put some hot ashes out from the night before.

He died of a heart attack, trying to put the fire out with a bucket of water. He might have survived, but he was on his own and was found when the Fire Brigade arrived, as the next door neighbour had called them because the fire had ignited again and caught a hold of the neighbour's fence as well.

In the morning me and my pal Jeff, who had travelled down to the funeral together, we were invited back to the Farmer's Rest for breakfast.

It's a lovely, quaint old country pub. I have a read of the morning papers, had forgotten about the horse I had put the bet on, then I remembered, go to the racing results page, blow me down, its only won at 3/1. £1,500 winnings. My pal Alan would have been proud of me, as he was the worst tipster in the world.

We went to Chester Races one day, he parked his car up, and we walked 100 yards when he said he needed to go back to the car. He opens the boot, pulls out the spare wheel, and then a bag of fifty pound notes.

He laughs and says the wife does not know about his little hideaway. It's from his after dinner speeches. I have to have some enjoyment, us laughing our heads off, as Leslie (wife) looked after all the finances, and she knew exactly what he was like.

He was always a happy go lucky little sod.

When he was manager of Manchester City, he lived in a beautiful village called Prestbury, about five miles outside Manchester, and when I went to visit him, he would say bring me some pies from McManus's.

It's a pie shop in Farnworth where we lived as kids, and believe me they are the best. I would take him six meat and six meat and potato. Class. We had loads of it, we even ate them on a plate with knives and fork, ha, ha. Naw only telling porkies.

We would just use our hands and have a big bite, and let the gravy run down our faces and hands .... magic.

Anyway, a month after the funeral in Southampton, there was

a special service in the Parish Church in Bolton in remembrance of Alan, all his friends and old Bolton Wanderers players, which I had arranged, were there and it was to be a happy day. Alan's children came up from Southampton, and his relations from Farnworth and Bolton were there.

There were various speeches including his Uncle Trevor Ball, who is one of my best pals. He was giving his speech, and he telling about myself and the great times we all had together. All of a sudden this mobile phone goes off, and me not being too clever with phones, suddenly realised it was mine.

It's only playing a hip-hop tune, which my daughter Samantha had put on as a ring tone for me. I thought it will go off soon, so I just sat there, pretending it was in somebody else's pocket. Eventually, I could not stand the tension any longer, stood up, took the call, and said to the speaker, Trevor, "I am sorry about this, but it's a very important call, it's Alan," the congregation are on edge and quiet.

"Alan just said could I bring him some pies from McManus's, in Farnworth. I told him they will be cold when I get there, oh no they wont, he said, you won't be that long behind me."

The Church erupted with laughter, it was a great day for my pal, who was a fantastic guy and I truly miss the fun and humour we shared, and I miss him more than anybody can imagine. He was just like my other pal, Wiggy who passed away years before, who I played football with in Ireland. God there's nothing better than being alive.

Bally and I went to Exeter Races with a friend of Alan's, who was an old farmer, Mr. Baker. He also had six horses in training, two were running that day in the 2.30pm. So Old Man Baker makes his way from the Paddock, to the bookmakers. He goes up to one of these bookies, it's a three horse race. Favourite is priced at 1/2, second favourite is 8/1 and the third horse is a 33/1 shot.

He says, "Could I have £200 on the one at 33/1, "Certainly sir. Thank you," was the reply. Our pal says: "Are you not rubbing that price out 33/1." "No," said the bookie, "I'll have another £200 at 33 to 1." Bet taken. The bookie then says, "Old man, I own that horse, you have put your money on." "Don't worry about it, I own the other two," said Old Man Baker.

The late Alan Ball, the Everton and England World Cup winner from 1966 showing how its done on Jim Good's well manicured lawn in Kinsale, Co. Cork. Again this photograph was taken a few months before 'Bally' passed away.

Relaxing in Kinsale, Co. Cork with best mates, Jim Good and the late Alan Ball

Alan Ball's Memorial Service in Bolton attended by, back left - Sid Faramond (ex-Bolton), Roy Hartle (Cup winner with Bolton in 1953), Mike Summerbee (Manchester City & England), Carl Davenport, the late Les Berry (well known in soccer & cricket circles in Bolton) & Francis Lee.

The Dav and the great Franny Lee, the ex-Bolton, Manchester City and England winger at Lee's home in Wimslow, Cheshire.The two lads joined Bolton Wanderers on the same day as 14 year olds and have been mates for over 50 years! The Dav featured in Lee's autobiography.

TRIP TO NEWCASTLE UNITED

The new season had just started in the Premiership, late August 2007, and my first trip up to see my old pal big Sam Allardyce who had just become the new manager up at Tyneside, after his magical feats at Bolton Wanderers, and just missing out on the England job. So off we go, myself, with Jeff and Russ Campbell. We call at Sam's house in Durham, Lynn, his wife and a lovely lady makes us a bite to eat, and Sam has to get to the ground early, to talk to his players, some people have to work.

Lynn gives us match tickets, and a ticket for the car park. We arrive at the ground one hour before the 3pm kick-off. We ask a steward where do we park the car, we drive up this spiral ramp, and before we know it we we're inside the stadium.

We lock the car and walk through this door, ask again where our seats are situated, we follow this gentleman, and he says, this is it. He opens the door, and there we are in the Royal Box, on the half way line, with free champagne and finger food all day and a gate of 58,000. Newcastle beat my old side Wigan Athletic that day and to his day my goal-scoring record of 48 goals in one season still stands, I think anyway.

I nearly said, I wish I were playing now, no I don't. I had the greatest time of all in the 60s - 70s and would not swap it for anything, money does not make you happy, but I was happy back then.

When the game ended, we were still having a drink and chatting about the game, and I remembered, we said we would go and meet Sam in his office.

Off we go, down to his office and I overheard him say to someone, "Go and look for that 'fucker' Dav, he was supposed to meet me." "I'm here," I said, everybody laughing. We had a few more drinks and off we went into the town centre, out of the 58,000 people at the match, 50,000 had black and white stripped shirts on, for the Magpies, and it was the same in town. Fanatical supporters, and lovely people in the North East of England, they really are.

Back to our hotel at 12.30am, a good day had been had by the three of us, so off to bed. In the morning, after breakfast, which we had overlooking the River Tyne, the hotel was called the Elephant on Tyne. Jeff and Russ, went back to St. James's Park as we had left the car there, only about 15 minutes in a taxi. I went back to our room for a hot bath and to be ready for the lads when they returned. As I have had heart problems in the past and taking 10 tablets a day, I also have a spray and if I feel any pain in the chest, I spray once under the tongue. If it does not work, you do it again. Thankfully I have never used it. Don't ask me why, but this time I did use it, six times? So, I get into the bath, I start to feel strange (yes, I always have been), so I pull the plug out of the bath just in case I might faint. I manage to get out of the bath, just got into the bedroom, and I collapse. As I was falling I must have grasped the trouser press, which was fixed to the wall, with my head underneath it. But that didn't straighten me out, ha, ha.

Anyway I manage to get myself onto the bed, and rang my pals, as I was lying there, my thoughts were, if I don't die, I will never drink, smoke, or go with women again.

I must have been very bad! My pals rang the ambulance, and the paramedics, who are fantastic people, said did I want an ECG at the hospital or would they do it here. I said here, so they did my blood pressure, which was 65, nearly dead, and they then wired me up for the ECG. That showed my heart was OK. When I told them about the spray, they knew immediately, what had gone wrong.

Well following a couple of hours rest, my blood pressure had recovered, and off we went on our three hour journey back to Bolton. Me, I'm on the back seat, in the position I would be if I were on a stretcher. The two lads, decide, after two hours driving they would like to stop for a drink at Ian Hosford's pub. He used to be a goalkeeper for Blackpool and for the England U21's, after Jeff and Russ had their few pints, they arrived out and what do you think they had for me, a bottle of Lucozade.

Thanks a million, what thoughtful friends I have, I could have been dead here in the back of the car, but still the thought was there.

SPORTS IN ENGLAND TODAY

Just a thought on the state of present day sport in England. We are a nation of not being any good at ball games, just to mention a few, soccer, cricket and tennis.

We used to be the best in the world, but now we are also rans, why? I will tell you. Up to the 1960s there was no TV, kids had to make their own entertainment, like playing sport, that includes being outside in the fresh air, not just sitting on their arses watching TV or playing with their PlayStations.

It's no surprise that this new word has appeared, OBESE. I didn't know what it meant until recently. Fat, to us older generation. Well, I will tell you how this disaster in sport started, from the late 70s, take football as an example, it stopped being played in schools all over Bolton, as there were no soccer coaches, the teachers, only one at my school, was interested in football, and he ran the school team. He was the Gardening Master, he was also getting near retirement age then, and after that – nothing. This was also the case all over the country. The game stopped being played in schools, it also happened with cricket and tennis. I was good at those sports, and have medals to prove it. You can play tennis socially in later life, and I have made a lot of friends, through playing all through my life. What I am saying, anything you play when your at school, don't give it up when you leave school. Keep playing, it keeps you fit, you meet people and you never know, if you keep practising and are dedicated enough, it's still not too late to make the big time. Somebody has to, and it might be you. I think I am drifting away from the subject, writers block, I think that's what they call it.

Oh yes, back to how it all went wrong. Coaching badges were introduced in the 1960s, what a farce, you could have been the best footballer in the world, but you had to have a badge, to coach or manage a team.

Well since then every Tom, Dick or Harry have got them. I know a school teacher, who I played tennis with for a local club in Bolton, he played soccer for a team called Old Sladonians, about the same standard as a pub team, this is 25 years ago, he's been the top coach in America for schoolboys ever since, amazing.

Bolton Wanderers and other Premier League clubs, have academies and employ people, because they have badges. It is no wonder there is no young talent coming through, I have forgotten more than they will ever know, so what a sad state we are in, and believe me it will get worse. I have talked to a lot of the so-called coaches at top level, and their ideas and tactics are from another planet.

They use all these new words, it would bamboozle a lot of people. It sounds good, modern, but what a load of crap. The tactics of skill, good tackling, and wanting to win, you cannot beat that in a team, formations go out the window if a player beats two men with his ball control. I am not going into this discussion, it makes me sad, the best eleven players will always win or the club with the most money. Going back to

104

the coaching badges, and how you get them, you would go on a course, be a top qualified man with all the badges he could accommodate, even though he might be a school teacher, or a plumber. My best pal Freddie Hill, ex-Bolton Wanderers, Manchester City and England, went to one of theses courses in the early 70s. There were a few good players there as well, the Head Coach said; "Fred, would you come forward," not having a clue who he was. Fred steps forward, in his long shorts, shirt and trainers, Coach says: "Would you try and kick that ball straight for five yards". Well the lads all started laughing, then one said, "He only played for England two days ago." I think that says a lot about coaches and their lovely badges, Bollicks!

WHERE IT ALL WENT WRONG

It was 1966, England had just won the World Cup, under Sir Alf Ramsey, a professor from Oxford. A friend of mine said, it's the worst thing that could happen to England, winning. I asked, why? Kids won't want to be wingers anymore, he said. You know he was dead right.

Wingers cross balls into the penalty area and that is where goals are scored from, correct.

Then as time moved on, the FA were providing coaching badges to people who had never kicked a ball, school teachers, anybody who had played, even who had never played the game. Football has been played for centuries, it's still the same rules, tactics are the same, they won't admit it, but believe me it is.

Tommy Docherty 'The Doc' once said if he had 10 of the best passers of a ball in the world, they would never lose a match. True.

Another way, the game has gone wrong. When we were kids

we had no television or video games. I lived in a terraced house with cobbled streets, a lamp post and tennis ball, and I would keep practising until my Mum or Dad shouted for me to come in for my supper. I took that tennis ball everywhere with me, that ball was my life as a kid.

I have got very strong thoughts on good friends, and surprisingly male ones. I don't think we show enough love. I love my pals, so why don't I tell them, am I afraid too, or is it just a stupid male thing.

I expect everybody to know how I feel, and should know, I should have married a mind reader. I think to tell the truth, be yourself, and help others where possible. These are great attributes, and you will not go far wrong in life. People say, I wish I had done this, I wish I had plenty of money, I wish I was me, as I would not have changed a thing, and I am still alive, what more could I wish for ?

Oh! A young 28-year-old, who would be a good cook, good with the Hoover and was OK in bed. Good job I have not changed a thing.

To conclude, I would like to be buried in Bolton, and my ashes scattered to the four winds at Charles Fort in Kinsale, Co. Cork. If you think about that plan, I don't think it's going to work, do you? Buried, burnt, would do well to get ashes out of being buried. I will let my children sort that out.

A FUNNY OLD GAME

Has the game changed? Who was the greatest? Very difficult questions. George Best, Messi, Tom Finney, Stanley Matthews, Pele, Maradona, Peter Doherty, Neil Franklin, David Jack, Hughie Gallagher, Tommy Lawton, Len Shackleton, Nat Lofthouse.

It is a question we will never know, style of play, better boots, better balls, training, pitches, more professional backroom staff.

In the past, everybody played football at school, at dinner time, and at home and went on until dark, and then I with my pals would carry on under the street lamps. Two or three of us would have a tennis ball, and dribble against each other, and hitting the lamp post was a goal. Just to make it that bit harder, the street was cobbled. It's no wonder everybody had skill in those days. We were brought up with it. We had nothing else to do with our time, but to play the greatest game in the world. No computer games, few had TVs, all we had was what normal boys and girls had and did what we were told by our parents. This is where it all went wrong.

You can play all the formations you want, but if anybody runs at a defender, and has the skill to beat a man, like years ago, then your formation has disappeared out the window. We have had over-lapping full backs, wing backs, what are we going to call them next, could be over flapping wing-backs, but it does look good for the coaches, more technical, my Dear Watson.

Another question which will never be answered, In years gone by in England, 50,000 to 60,000 at every match, where did the money go?

It was not spent on players, they were home-grown, not on the ground improvements, the directors did have big houses and fancy cars, it might have gone there?

Professional and amateur, people say is there much difference, Yes, a bottom professional will always be better than a top amateur. That gap will always be there. In nearly every sport, if you get to a professional level, you are the best because the rest have not made the cut, just like golf.

Having said that, a lot of people are good at some sport at school, as soon as they leave they don't follow it up, or start smoking, drinking, girls, it sounds all right to me.

JOKES AND THE COIN TRICK

It has always been my way to entertain on and off the field, because I enjoyed doing it so much. I love company, and always wanted everybody to be happy, tell jokes or stories, what would just come into my mind at that moment. I have a great memory for things like that, but football matches, no. It was said that I didn't get fresh jokes, I got a new clubs where they had not heard them before. The party piece trick I always did, and I have done it in a lot of countries, was flicking a coin up in the air and catching it on my foot, then off my foot and onto the back of my head. I could do it drunk or sober. Practice and timing, that's the secret. People would try this and I would give them as many goes as they wanted. They never did it. It originated from my days at Preston North End in 1961. Two players there, Alan Spavin and Colin Alty and myself, in the dinner break between training sessions, we would be practising and I still do it, 40 years on. No problem. I have met a lot of people years on and they always say: "I remember you doing that trick with the coin". Nothing about the hundreds of goals I scored. That's life!

I had a particular trick on the football field. My Dad showed me and taught it to me when I was about 10-years-old. It was to run with the ball, put a leg over it at speed. The ball was still where it was and the other leg would drag it with me, at the pace I was moving at. Simple but very effective as your opponent was watching the ball, and you had gained a yard past him.

They all fell for that one! In Ireland, this had never been seen before and I christened it 'The Bolton Palais Shuffle' as when I lived in Bolton earlier in my life, that's where I went dancing. Rock and Roll in those days. Francis Lee, myself and another Bolton player, Charlie Cooper. He was a full-back, so he struggled with the shuffle. Myself, Charlie, Freddie Hill, the England international, my best pal, and Bob Green. We played snooker every week together to this day. Bob Green used to watch me play when I was 13 years old for Farnworth Boys Club. His uncle, Eric Green ran our team, but Bob, who is an artist, moved to Dublin. When I played over here he came and watched me play a lot of games and can tell me about the goals. I cannot remember, but he never introduced himself to me until 20 years later in Bolton. That is amazing. I asked why ? He said he was too shy as I was a celebrity. I said: "Celebrity my ass. I am still 'the Dav' and always will be".

When driving from the ferry in Dublin, as I go through Mitchelstown and up the hill, at the top is a lovely pub called the Gloccamaura Inn. A nice man called Denis Nolan owned it. His son of the same name was in digs with me on Mardyke Walk as he was at school nearby.

All this time I am getting nearer Cork City, and I always get excited. Through Fermoy and when I see the sign 'Land of the Dixies' I think "God, I am nearly home". If Joe Mac could see me now, as I usually sing to myself. I am that happy.

My mind suddenly goes into memory alert. All the great memories come flooding back; how it was like in the late 60s.

I am getting carried away with nostalgia. I am in the past. Then I look into the driver's mirror. It cannot be me I see. It looks like my grand dad. That quickly brings me back to the reality of being an old person. Forget that, I still feel 28!

RAY DAVIES, THE KINKS & THE CAROUSEL

The best club I ever signed for was The Carousel Night Club, in Cork. They only played night matches and they were all played at home. Wages, none. Certified girls, plenty, scored five one night with about an hour in between each goal!

Just enough time to get my breath back. I am still the leading scorer with well over two thousand ! That's up to the present day, but I think my career is getting near the end. I will soon have to hang my trousers up!

In the Carousel, they played a lot of The Kinks music and in later years Ray Davies married Pat, who was sister to my then wife, Jean. Ray was the lead singer of the group. My other brother-in-law was my friend Jim Good of Kinsale. Well, we all got divorced and set up our own group, The Kinkies. We did not sell many albums but we did top the charts with 'You Win Again', a record which Hot Chocolate bought off us, and sang years later and went to Number One again. The old ones are the best. Well we were, but time catches up with you. We are into hang gliding now. It's much safer!

LIVING LONGER, SPAIN

Talking about people going abroad for their holidays, a lot of people from Britain are going to live in Spain, and it's a fact, with the clean fresh air and sun, they are living a lot longer and ailments seem to go away. Two of my best friends, David and Pat Higham moved over there 20 years ago, and believe me, it's put 10 years extra on their lives.

Our pals, Lyne and Sam Allardyce live next to them and will end up living there permanently when Big Sam retires from football. I hope it's soon as I have had to ring him up the day before the game to give him my team selection, and this puts a lot of pressure on me, as I don't get paid. I told Sam that my doctor said that this was doing me no good since the heart problems and that I would be much better drinking, smoking and going with women. He said, "What's your doctor's name?" I said "Crippin." He was the guy who murdered half his patients. Just a bit of good news for heart attack victims who have survived, like myself. Keep taking the tablets. My pal Alan Ball never got the chance. We are very lucky.

SPORT, BONFIRE NIGHT

Gone are the days, when teenagers filled in their free time with sport, even walking in the countryside, and smells of nature's aromas of plants, trees and beautiful scenery, going to the cinema and a bag of chips on the way home.

In the street where I lived, everybody looked after each other, neighbours were like family. The street would organise a coach trip, every September, to the Blackpool Illuminations, which was an hour away from our house.

Bonfire night was another great time in my young life, collecting wood, old furniture, anything that would burn on the fire. Mushy black peas, red cabbage, home chestnuts and bonfire toffee (treacle) and the fireworks, of course, jack-jumpers, rockets, flares. They were great times. All the families sat around the fire, talking, laughing, telling stories of their childhood, and the contentment on their faces, and the past memories of their bonfire nights when they were children.

CHANGES IN TIME

It's strange how things change in a lifetime – no television, so people went to the cinema, a great night out. Capitals of countries have changed, even the names of countries and all cars were different shapes, with chrome bumpers. Now they are all the same shape and no character. Soccer players had a good relationship with the fans, and would go in their local pubs for a drink after a game. It does not happen today as they have too much money and are on a different level to ordinary people. That's sad. Today, nobody should be dressed scruffy. Clothes are cheaper than they have ever been. But we have become a very untidy and shabbily dressed nation.

What will it be like in another 20 years or so I dread to think. Drink, drugs, and crime, they are all connected but they don't get punished enough. Prison is too good for them. Put them in the army for two years. That will sort them out. I know quite a lot of the personnel and they would soon straighten them out as these people don't know the word discipline. I cannot imagine how they were brought up and what their parents think about them.

SOCIAL

Life has it's highs and lows. To have money is great. To have no money at some stage in your life is good. Why? It makes you learn the value of it.

Every penny counts and when you have been in that position, you have been in the real world. Anybody who tells you differently, doesn't have a clue.

I think that idea of saving up and accumulating as much as possible, as people did years ago, are gone. Today's society spends on holidays, cars, home comforts and dining out. None of this was done by the older generation, as all they wanted to do was to save if possible, and then leave it to their children who would blow it immediately.

I think times have changed, and parents are doing things more. They are going places, new car, and are looking younger and healthier than past generations. So, as all these parents of 50 plus lived respectable lives, most will not go out after dark, in towns or cities, as violence, drug culture, drunkenness and robberies are all too prevalent.

I have only just learned of the phrase: 'Hoodies' in recent times but I say put them in the Army for 12 months. That will sort them out. If that doesn't work, there's always the electric chair!

DENIS IRWIN & A CHANCE MEETING

I met Denis Irwin of Manchester United and Ireland in a tennis village complex just outside Bolton a few years ago.

He's originally from Cork, from Togher to be precise, and a lot younger than me. So when I was playing in Cork, Denis was brought to the games by his father, Justin.

Each and every home game they came and watched me play.

He started to tell me that I was his hero in those days and could not believe that it's taken all those years for us to meet.

It made me feel good, and I told him so. Denis had a fantastic career with Man United. He played left-back and was a model of consistency, winning European Cups, FA Cups and league titles, plus a regular with his country.

WHAT HAPPENED TO THE GAME
Old Boots

The ball is a very special thing in a footballer's life. You spend every day with it, and it almost becomes part of you. And when you make a pass, you have to caress it, and when you shoot at goal, get your body over the ball and your head down, just like a golfer when he takes a shot. It's exactly the same principle for a footballer.

If you're running at a defender with the ball, the easiest way to beat him is to drop one shoulder, as if you were going left of him, and with the outside of your right foot, go the opposite way. It's easy and you're travelling at pace and the defender is standing still. Yes, it is that easy.

The only thing that has changed dramatically are the actual boots. They had big, solid toecaps, a big broad band across the instep and very high up the ankles. Also, made of tough leather, you had to stand in water for a few hours to break them in. It actually took a month before you could play in them. When they were ready to play matches in, after a month, the studs had to be changed. These were leather, three nails in them. You would take the old ones off, put them on an iron cast, a three-pronged invention for resoling shoes, shaped like the Isle of Man. You would hammer these studs in. They were shaped like a thimble. The nails would go through the sole and bend inside the sole. They were very secure until, during a game when one of the nails would go into your foot. Then you would move faster, to the touchline where the trainer would fix it with the hammer.

In today's game, these so-called 'players' would be off to hospital. Shin-guards have always been part of a footballer's kit. When I started playing at a competitive level, like schoolboy football, and knowing my future was going to be a professional soccer player, my Dad always made me wear them. They were about eight inches long and five inches wide. The back of them was foam. Inside of that there were four long pieces of cane, to protect your shins. My Dad did not think that good enough. He added a roll of cotton wool onto the foam back and also made me wear a small pair of shin guards on the outside of my legs, near the ankles. I never got any injuries. Dad was just looking after my future, as he always did, but when I took them off after a game, I found I was that fast, I was always at the bar first, with both my shins intact.

As you know, footballers invariably come from a working class background. It was the only sport played at school. That's where all the talent came from. Rugby, cricket and tennis players came from private education, universities. There is nothing wrong with that, and I don't think it has changed much today. They are all sports and you have a choice of which sport you want to play.

COLTS TO THE FIRST TEAM

Years ago, take Bolton Wanderers for instance, they only had two old scouts, Frank Pickford and Arthur Nash. These two alone brought all the top young hopefuls from a 40-mile radius in Lancashire to Bolton Wanderers.

Clubs then never bought players like today. They were home grown. They would start in the Colts, the youngest team, B team next, A team next, then the reserves, and then the magical first team. And that's how it worked. What happened next was, most likely, the most stupid thing ever to take place among football clubs, was that they scrapped their C, B and A teams. Why? To save money. What a joke!

Instead of the system they had of having five teams, and home grown players working their way up through the ranks to the first team, for the sake of £10,000 a year, it has cost them billions of pounds, by having to buy players who are over-paid, and are not up to the job.

I am not saying all of them, but one bad buy could have kept the home grown players coming through the old system for years. If you were a business man, I know which one you would go for. And so would any other person in his right mind. You don't have to be a genius to work it out. How sad! I cringe as I am writing this and this just goes to show in my writing earlier, T.V. PlayStations, no school football.

SCORING GOALS

How to score goals and why they can't today. First of all, you have to be a bit selfish. Make space for yourself, not be afraid to shoot on sight, and run into the space where you think that ball will go. That gives you that extra yard on your opponent. It's called 'instinct', a very valuable asset. Forwards want that extra touch on the ball, instead of getting their shot in first time. And that's a lack of confidence. The more you shoot with power, the more goals you will score. They might not all hit the target, but the ones that do, have a good chance of hitting the back of the net.

And to finish, a great goal-scorer has to be brave, to put his body on the line and his head where nobody else would - in where the boots fly.

In today's modern game, there are not too many great headers of the ball. I learned from one of the best the world has seen, the great Nat Lofthouse at Bolton Wanderers.

I spent hours practising with the great man, heading the ball. It is all down to timing the jump and when you get in the air, you stay there. Your neck muscles tighten, your head comes back and then forward, and meeting the ball with your forehead, it leaves your head like a bullet. But to master the art, you have to practice for hours and most players will never be able to do that. Denis Law was a master at it.

So, if you have not got all these attributes, or you think I am wrong, get an office job and stop wasting your time!

THE PROFESSIONAL – PAST AND FUTURE

In my time in Ireland, it was like being in a magic ball. Time started to stand still as if I was in the middle of a fantastic beautiful dream, of sea and countryside and long, winding roads. And every road led to happy times. *"In dreams you're mine, all the time, together in dreams,"* the Big O. Everybody has special periods in their life and you only realise that when you stop and think back and say to yourself, yes, it was such a time. And you smile and say, yes it was great.

An awful lot of people who say I should have done this and should have done that, they are the ones who most likely have never been happy, accomplished nothing, or greedy, and they wanted to have more money than they have up-to-date. Very sad! You only get dealt the cards once, no dummy runs.

As for myself, if anybody asks me, what would you have done differently, my reply is, I would not change a thing. I have had everything, a career in football of 20 odd years, great friends, lovely family, done my own thing, and I am still alive, Thank God.

What on earth could I have done better?

In 1969 a strange thing happened to me. I had gone to see a friend of mine who owned a pub, near the South Infirmary, called the Commodore, it was later the Whiff & Poof and it's Paddy the Farmer's now.

His name was Mex Donovan. He used to be the head steward on the Innisfallen, which in those days was the ferry from Fishguard to Cork and that probably was how the Welcome Wales Week started in the city.

And, as I am on the subject, I honestly cannot believe that there has never been a ferry for years. It's as if Cork didn't want tourists any more and flights are also expensive so I was delighted to see the return of the Cork- Swansea ferry and I am happy to say that I have been a passenger on it already.

The moral of this story is Dublin seems to take all the tourists, hen parties, 21st parties, and our dear old beautiful city gets nothing. I think you should vote for me in the next election, as I have been on about this for over 20 years. Vote now, at least, you will get some action. And I am always for the working class. Oh yes! Back to the Commodore. Sorry I drifted, but it's an important fact.

So I have had a chat with Mex, as there were not many in the bar. I then go and sit down at a table with my pint and cigar and this old well-dressed man said, "May I join you?"

I said, "Pull up a chair".

I had never met him before in my life, but I was about to learn amazing things about me, life, my future and my past. We got talking and he was a Professor at one of the Dublin colleges and coming up to retirement.

He said he knew all about me, but my mind questioned that and the talk and discussions went on for over an hour. It was very interesting and we had another couple of drinks and then this magical statement of seeing into the future came out of his mouth.

My jaw dropped. He said that England winning the World Cup would be a disaster for English football.

"Why?" I asked.

"Well, they played without wingers, so no kids will want to be wingers anymore. Also that formation will never win anything again".

Well, he was right, and 40 years have passed and he's still spot on. The only team that wins is Manchester United with the likes of Ronaldo and Giggs, both out and out wingers.

His next prophecy was that people who have their own business will make a lot of money as labour will be so cheap.

119

Yes, that has happened also.

And foreigners have moved over from their own countries to work for less and do the jobs that the local people will not do. True again.

I have just a little story to tell you and everybody thought it very obvious in 1970. This small boat was bound for Britain with 500 Vietnamese on board. It approaches Southampton Docks and a voice shouts from the boat. "Ahoy there".

Voice shouts back from the jetty, "What are you carrying".

"500 Vietnamese boat people", was the reply.

Voice back from jetty, "Sorry. Try Fleetwood".

Another day and a half up to Fleetwood. But the same thing happens there, but they are told to "Try Ireland".

Well, after three more days at sea, the passengers were in a terrible state, and it had become a very unhealthy environment. They eventually arrive at Ballycotton, Co. Cork. Voice on the front of the boat shouts out: "Ahoy there".

Voice shouts back of the end of the wooden jetty. "Ahoy there. What are ye carrying?"

Reply, "500 Vietnamese boat people".

Voice shouts back, "Are they on pallets?"

Getting back to the third prophesy, he looked at me straight in the eyes, as if looking inside my head. Then he said, "You have done everything" (I thought here we go. He means women). "You have lived in the fast lane all your life and there's not much left you have not done. And by the time you're 50, you will be bored with the time you will have left".

And I have to say he is not far wrong in many ways. I only lived with my two boys Mark and Jason for five years and they have lived in America for 20 years.

Of course, we visit each other, but I miss them a lot. My daughter Samantha, I only lived for five years with her, as me

120

and her mother split up. We never married. Samantha lives near me in Bolton and but for her, I would be alone.

But all three of my children are fantastic and I can tell you this, it was the best thing ever to happen to me, and I love them dearly. But they all have that bit of 'the Dav' in them, and all like a good laugh. Also they are all very close to each other. I am a lucky sod!

Getting back to the professor, he was like Merlin. He just got up from his chair in the bar, put his overcoat on, then the trilby, shook my hand and said: "Always remember me. I will never see you again but I might, in another lifetime", and disappeared out the door. When Mex had time to talk to me, I told him what had gone on with the gentleman I had been sitting with.

Mex just said: "Every time I looked over you were on your own"!

Last man standing
left to right - Alan Ball Senior who managed Preston and Halifax, his son
England star Alan, Jeff Cordell Manager of Maxwell Plums, Big Nick assistant Manager
and a dapper-looking Dav

Carl back in his beloved Kinsale and outside the Trident Hotel with
from left to right; Cara Cowhie, Jim Good and Ray Cowhie

TALL TALES
Being The Gaffer

As you have read, I was the youngest ever professional manager at the age of 23 and was successful. My training methods were very advanced and also tactics, even after training, pulse rates would be checked and monitored and on Fridays all the players were called to a meeting.

I had my Big Red Book with me, which had last week's performances, how they had done in training during the week and so on and then I would announce the team that would take to the field the following day.

I remember my first team meeting. It went on for about half-an-hour and I asked, "Have you any questions you want to ask me".

Oh yes! There is always one smart Alec. Yes!

"Dav, you have not mentioned yourself".

"Very observant", I say. "Well done!"

I look at them all sitting down around the room. I stand up and I say, "When we are anywhere near the opposition penalty area, you pass the ball to me".

Silence around the room, then a voice says, "Why?"

My reply: "I am the manager, the best player and I am the one, and the only one, who's going to score any fucking goals, and if you don't give me the ball, you will not be playing next week. Thank you very much and I will see you tomorrow and don't forget the plan".

BOBBY TAMBLING - PAINTING JOB

When I played in the 1974 League winning team with Cork Celtic, I scored three goals in the last three games that won us the league title, and that was how I met Bobby Tambling, the ex-Chelsea and England player and Chelsea's most celebrated goal scorer of all time.

Bobby became manager of Celtic the following season and lived in Kinsale where I'd been too. And we both played darts for the Spaniard pub team, so we spent a lot of time together and became good friends.

At the time, Bobby was a Jehovah's Witness and my wife then, Jean, was very interested in the way it worked, but after a couple of months Bobby said to me, "Would you like to be a Witness?".

I said that I never saw the accident. That was the end of that for both of us.

A couple of years later, I had a painting and decorating business and had got a school to paint in Killeagh, through a good friend of mine Stephen, who was a farmer and was the man behind Killeagh soccer team, where I ended up playing, along with Ray Cowhie.

I got paid £50 per week which was good money then. All I had to do was to score three or more every week. That was like shelling peas. So everybody was happy and the drink flowed after every game.

So, back to painting the school. It was a big job, so I asked Bobby if he would help me and that he would have to stay down with me, a few nights, as it was too far to travel each day.

So I booked a room for us, at the Sir Walter Raleigh in Youghal, a nice place, I might add. The first day we started the job I picked Bobby up in Kinsale. I had a gold coloured

Jaguar at the time and as we got into Cork, I pulled over to the side of the road, our back door opened and in gets this fantastic girl, legs up to her armpits, a real stunner.

I said to Bobby, "This is Jenny, a friend of mine. She's staying in Youghal with us a couple of days".

Still shocked, he just said, "OK".

I cannot remember the sleeping arrangements but we only had one room and that wasn't for praying.

Buzz O'Connell of Crosshaven with Carl, Donal O'Flynn and England & Chelsea legend Bobby Tambling after the 'Dav's testimonial with Bolton Wanderers in Rosie's Bar in Carrigaline, Co. Cork.

Centre-forwards United! The great Nat Lofthouse of England & Bolton Wanderers with Carl at Nat's old haunt the 'Cheetham Arms' in Edgeworth, Bolton. Nat was known as the 'Lion of Vienna' after a famous England victory over Austria and the Dav was groomed to be his protégé.

WASHING DAY IN BOLTON

When I was a kid in Bolton, I lived in a terraced house. We had a backyard and a back street and Monday of every week was washing day. Thousands of clothes lines across every back street in Lancashire were full of clean, white washing. Coal men with their heavy sacks and dustbin men, they all had their own day of the week. Don't forget, there were no washing machines. It was all hand-washed, with soap and a scrubbing board.

Coalmen would carry the heavy sacks and tip them in the coal shed, and a bin man would come around the day before collecting, and put your metal bin outside your back gate, ready for the collection.

How things have changed, and not for the better. We had two beautiful theatres, The Grand and The Theatre Royal. Great artists appeared there, Charlie Chaplin, Harry Houdini and many more famous names. Temperance bars opened, that's non-alcoholic drinks. These people said that drink was the curse of the working man, and in Bolton in those days, there were loads of cotton mills, and 70% of the townspeople would be employed in them, and with no televisions, the pub was a great place to go and have a chat or play dominoes or darts.

Or to a football match on Saturday's at Burnden Park, the home of Bolton Wanderers where you could guarantee 50,000 people at every home match.

And there was never any trouble. People were happy, even though they had not much money. Why can't it be like that in today's society?

CARS & THE TROUBLE THEY CAN GET YOU INTO

When I was 17 I passed my driving test and bought a Ford Cortina WBN 678. It was maroon and brand new right out of the showroom.

I was playing for Preston at the time and me and my pal, Steve Fagan used to get in all sorts of scrapes. I needed new tyres after 10,000 miles, Oh yes! I was reckless. I would go around roundabouts the wrong way at 3am in the morning.

I still had the car when I moved to play for Stockport County. One week before Christmas we had a players' party after we had done our training, at a little old pub, not far from the ground.

This old landlady called Doris, a lovely lady ran the pub. We started drinking at 1pm. Boddington's Bitter. It's like rocket fuel. By 4pm we were rocking. Doris says to me: "Would you move my car?" as it was over the cellar trap door outside and the dray men had arrived from the brewery and they wanted to get the full wooden barrels down into the cellar.

So I moved the car, and they carried on, rolling the beer down the ramp. By this time a couple of players had come out to see what was going on. We were so drunk, one tried to lift one into the boot of my car. There was no chance. It was too heavy and the boot was nowhere near big enough, but at least we tried!

At about 6pm, me and my pal John Wylie – he was club captain – decided we should head home, and he did not drive and his house was on the way, so I gave him a lift. It was absolutely throwing it down with rain. We were going down this steep main road, and at the front of us is a bread van. All of a sudden he brakes. I do the same, but mine don't work.

Bang, at speed, into the back of him. Smoke comes out of my bonnet, what was left of it, and using the handbrake, I finally get the car to stop. But the large bread van carries on, and into the distance, and disappears into the night. Yes, I was in the wrong, drinking and never getting the brakes checked, but what about the driver of the bread van?

Bread men finish delivering at dinner time and with it being around Christmas time, he also must have had a few drinks. Another lucky escape! My car was a write-off and so nearly were we.

A couple of weeks later, after the insurance claim, I said the brakes had failed and no-one else was involved. As you do! I bought another new car, a Zephyr 4, the model had just come out and was in the showroom. Again it was Goodwood Green, bench seats and column change. It was the business. I drove it out of the showroom. My Dad was with me and we drove home. We felt like millionaires. The smell of a new car is something special. When we arrived home, my Mum had the tea ready and we all sit down to eat. At the end of the meal, I say "I am going out later to meet a friend". Yes it was a young lady, but they did not know that as they thought I never bothered with the opposite sex!

I was a young footballer and that was bad for me, as stated earlier. I got dressed after a bath and shave, get into my new car. It had been bad weather. Not really wanting to get the car dirty, off I went to pick my date up for the night.

We decide to go for a drink and the rain is still lashing down and I did not want to be late home as I was training the following day. So we left the pub early and I decided to take her home. Getting near her house, sex getting the better of me again, I decided to find a quiet spot to stop. I see a small turning off the road ahead. I pull in and go along a small dirt track. I park the car, have a kiss and a cuddle, get our clothes off and there's a bump, but we carry on regardless.

Next thing I know, water is up to the top of the seat. The

ground underneath the car had given way and we were surrounded by water. "Oh no," I thought. "Brand new car, first day out of the showroom. What the hell am I going to tell my Dad !

My date got out of the window. It was no use dressing, bra and knickers were perfect in those conditions. And off she went home, like a channel swimmer. I had to ring Dad from a phone box and he rang a man with a tractor to get the car out.

When I arrived home, by taxi, I told my Dad, that I was taking a short cut and explained what had happened.

In the morning, I went to pick the car up. It started immediately and I drove it back home. But it was saturated inside and the rubber plugs underneath the carpets had been taken out to get rid of the water. What can I tell the garage, was my main concern.

Oh! I told them there were no plugs in it, and it was the manufacturers who were to blame. So they admitted they were to blame and redid the inside of the car. And all new carpets. But who else would that happen to, on the first day of driving a brand new car, only me !

HAMBURG & MACCESFIELD CIRCA 1965

When I played with Macclesfield Town, my pal was Billy Myerscough, a centre-forward who was coming to the end of his career, as he had, years before, played at Wembley for Aston Villa against the great Manchester United with Villa winning 2–1. Peter McFarland, a Northern Ireland international, scored the winning goal by shoulder charging the goalkeeper, Harry Gregg, into the back of the net.

Controversial yes, but that's how it was in those days. But Billy ended up with a Cup winners medal and it could not have gone to a nicer fellow.

So, after the season came to an end at Macclesfield and me notching 50 goals, winning the league as well, we decided on a two-week holiday to Hamburg, as Billy had been once before when on tour with Aston Villa. He was a good friend of Uwe Seeler, a German World Cup winner, who lived there.

Billy said we would go in his car and it was a Volkswagen Beetle, and if anything went wrong it would be OK as it was German made (you knew that anyway). We arrived by ferry, all excited. I think the naughty ladies of Hamburg had a lot to do with it. We found a cheap – call it a guest house – and we were in the Celler. Yes it was a hole. The next night Billy says, "We will get dressed up and I will take you to the classiest brothel in the world. It's called The Café Reece. It's the most famous. It's like nothing you will ever see again."

I could not wait. As we approached, a doorman opened the door for us and into the most beautiful room I had ever seen. It was like a palace. The décor was unbelievable and the most gorgeous ladies I have ever seen, all sitting at tables, some on their own, and more sat in twos. Billy says, "Which shall we have".

"I don't know", I replied. "Give me five minutes", as they were all film stars. Believe me, we had never seen anything like it and never have since. That's some statement from me! Eventually I said, "Those two over there", and over we went.

They stood up to introduce themselves. Simone, she was Swedish, obviously unbelievable (that was mine), Angar, Billy's one, was German. She would be with a name like that. But she was also a cracker.

We then get down to the business side of how much is it going to cost us. And don't forget I was only 22 at the time, plenty of experience but not a lot of money. £20 each was the answer. So, after a couple of bottles of champers, off we went to this hotel, about 100 yards away, and to our rooms, which were in with the fee which we had paid them.

What a time we had! I'm in love in five minutes! Well, I won't go into details but I was at it longer than I had paid for, and Simone said, "You're fantastic, and I am with older men mostly, and you young boy". (She would be about twenty six). "And I will meet you tomorrow. Cost you nothing".

Oh I am chuffed now. Can't wait for tomorrow. If only I knew what was to come! As we walked back to the Café Reece where I had said I would meet Billy, arm-in-arm with the glowing Simone, a gentleman came the other way and as he passed us, Simone put her hand into his and off they went. I have heard of love at first sight, but that was ridiculous. How naive I was at the time but it was worth every penny and that was the first and the last time, I ever paid for it.

Well, as I approached Billy waiting outside, the poor man had been waiting half an hour, so we went for a coffee and discussed our exploits.

It turned out that Angar preferred it backwards, nothing special in that. Whatever turns you on. "Oh," I said to Billy, "Look back in Angar", a famous film years ago with Dirk Bogart. Well, we cried laughing and I have always laughed whenever I think of that famous night in the city of Hamburg.

Just to finish off this tale, the third night of our trip we went out for a few drinks to a nice hotel, for a change. We met up with a few English people and I ended up taking a lovely looking girl back to our cellar. I should have stayed in the hotel with her but back we went. We had been in bed about half an hour, light on, and I looked up at the picture of a lady on the wall. Then I see one of her eyes move. It's the dirty, little old man who owned the place. It's a wonder he didn't fall off the box he was standing on, in the next room!

ALAN BALL SENIOR

When Alan Ball Senior was first team coach at Stoke City, he recommended me to the then manager of Cork Celtic, Mr. Bill Higgins, in late November of 1966, in which England won the World Cup by beating Germany at Wembley and young Alan Ball collecting his winner's medal. When I signed for Celtic in January 1967, after a few weeks, I and some of the players realised that Bill knew little about football and had never played the game. We used to throw the ball to him in training for a laugh and them legs had never played football. They were like two table legs. I could head it further than he could kick it. The strange thing was, he was quite a nice man, but followed me everywhere, and would want to listen and pick up knowledge of the game from me, and I was glad to help him. I think that was because he also liked the ladies and we would often visit the Rob Roy, as we knew the manager and the chef.

Ray Cowhie and Timmy (Becket) Murphy would also join us. Ray called him Henry Higgins out of My Fair Lady. Another of our meeting places was The Market Bar which was very posh in those days. Mossie, the barman knew of the team, as later after a match I would take all the players in to have a drink and discuss the game, while it was still fresh in our minds, and talk face to face with your team-mates and not behind their backs.

Getting back to the charming Bill, he had taken Cork Celtic from bottom of the league to safety, with a little help from yours truly, with 14 goals in 13 games, since I arrived in January. Bill got the sack at the end of the season. It was not through football, but the fact that he was not Bill Higgins, who played with Bolton Wanderers, as the real one had died years before, and the man was, well we don't really know, but what he was selling, as he always had a car boot full of the pill, yes, the one that stops you getting pregnant!

Well, in 1967 they weren't legal in Britain and definitely not in Ireland. Nobody ever heard of him again. He just disappeared. He could have taken too many of his own pills!

I took over as player manager the following season. Gates got very big, 15,000 at every home game. Our directors, John Horgan, Paddy Barry and Richie Neville, were happy for a change, and to top it off we finished runners-up in the League.

So, Bill disappeared into the night and most of his pills. My ladies never got pregnant and I never put on any weight. So thank you Bill for that, and I will always remember you as the man who never was.

Alan Ball Senior was an excellent coach and a man who would always be your pal. He was one of the first qualified coaches in Britain. He did not just have all the badges, but knew the game inside out. That was the main reason his son made it to be the one of the top players in the world. He started his managerial career at Stoke City, as head coach, to the then manager, Tony Waddington, the man who brought back Stanley Matthews from Blackpool, back to his home town club, where he started his footballing career as a twenty year old, and now was fifty. He was one of the greats of all time. Stan brought crowds back to Stoke, and in his first season back they won promotion back to the First Division. Stan died a few years ago. His statue is outside the ground. They called him *The Wizard of Dribble*. When he played for Blackpool he won a Cup Final with them against Bolton Wanderers in 1953. The great Nat Lofthouse was in the Bolton team that day, but Blackpool won 4 – 3. A little inside forward, Ernie Taylor, was Stan's inside partner and between them they tore Bolton's defence to pieces. But it will always be remembered as the Matthews' Final. That No. 7 shirt of Stan's was worn later by my pal, young Alan Ball. He wore it in his very first game against Liverpool. As I stated earlier, three days before that game, Alan was wishing he was me, as I was doing great at Preston and scoring plenty of goals in their reserve team, that's the second team. Alan was in Blackpool's fifth team, the Colts, but there had been a lot of injuries to players, and he got his chance. I wonder why he wanted to be me? I know, and so did he, that luck can be a great factor, not just in football, but in life, as you will find out when you read on!

Back to Father Ball. After doing a good job as coach at Stoke, before he left he fixed me up with Cork Celtic and guaranteed them that I would get them a goal a game, and that they had *The Playboy of the Western World,* all rolled into one. And I did not let him down on both counts. In fact, his name for me, if he introduced me to anybody, was "Meet *The Count of Cork*" and then with a wry smile he would say, "Some people misinterpreted it!"

He then went on to manage Preston, got them promotion and half way through the following season, had a minor heart attack and lost his job. He managed Halifax Town after that and had spells managing in Sweden.

Now the bad luck started for the family on New Year's Eve, 1985. I was having a party at my house in Farnworth, just outside Bolton and Alan turned up with his pal Paul Mann. The place was packed. The beer could not come out of the barrels fast enough, plus wine, women and song. Gone midnight, Alan informed me that he was off to Cyprus in the morning, to a coaching job there, and if he decided to take the job, would I like to join him and help him run the team? I just said, "Let's see what happens first, and then talk to me again".

He never talked to me again, as when the director of the club in Cyprus picked him up at the airport, Alan did not know the director was intoxicated and within three miles the car went around a bend and into a small ravine and into a dried up river bed.

Alan was pronounced dead immediately. The driver had not a mark on him but was later arrested for manslaughter.

Alan's wife Val, a lovely lady, who had been over with him many times when I lived in Cork, was never the same after his death, and passed away years later. That left young Alan and his wife Leslie, a fantastic lady, also a great friend. She was the strong one of the family, and ran all Alan's football business, but sadly, Leslie got cancer and fought it for three years. She lost the battle in the end.

Myself and Alan came over to Cork for a couple of weeks, to get his mind off things. We had a great time, playing golf, then a few days in Kinsale and Killarney, and it seemed to have helped him, but when he returned home, you don't know how people react behind closed doors, on their own. Alan died eighteen months later, of a heart attack, and even today I still cannot believe he's gone. I am still very sad and cannot forget him. He is survived by three lovely children; Jimmy, who will carry on with his Dad's soccer academies, and sisters Kylie and Mandy, and I do understand why Alan wanted to be me. I am still alive!

I know myself and Bally were close, but also in another way, our initials, A.B. / C.D., how unusual was that! I remember Alan and his father driving down to London and on the motorway five miles out of the City, they see a Rolls Royce stopped on the hard shoulder. They recognise it immediately. It was George Best and his chauffeur. So they slow down and pull up in front of them. "What's up George? You broken down?"

George says: "I have an important appointment in London in

half an hour".

"Don't worry", says Alan. "We will tow you in".

"No thanks", says George.

Could you imagine the headlines in the papers the next day? George Best towed into London by the Balls !

CROSSHAVEN

I used to go down to Crosshaven a lot when I was with Cork Celtic. In fact, I met a lovely girl who lived down there, called Mary. She was blonde, hair cut short and very stunning. We were great friends for a long time. There were quite a lot of things happened to me in Crosshaven over the years. My pal and soccer player Sydney Venner, who played with me in my very first game for Cork Celtic at Flower Lodge in January 1967, always and still does, live there.

I met Kelly of the Nevada Showband, at the Majorca dance hall, where she was singing. I liked Kelly and we became good friends, to say the least! I remember at the beginning of one season playing for Celtic, it had been a very hot summer. I got tackled near the half way line and I am lying face down to the ground. This voice shouts out of the crowd, "No wonder you're brown Dav, up and down on Kelly all summer, down in Crosser." The crowd howled with laughter. Another time somebody shouted, "Get up Dav, she's gone".

Cork wit ... you can't beat it. The crowds then were fantastic. 18,000 people. It was my pleasure to entertain them. Cork people are witty and enjoy the craic. No trouble with fans in those days. It was a Sunday afternoon out for the Dads and their kids. I am glad I did not miss that wonderful era.

Finally, at the end of my career, I played for Crosshaven, for half a season, again with my pal Sydney and another good player, Buzz O'Connell, a left-winger. I scored too many goals for them and before I knew it I was being transferred back to Cork Celtic and helped them win the league. So, Crosshaven was good for me, and I have great memories of it, except for being shot at, which I mentioned earlier in dispatches. You would not be reading anything at all if he had hit the target... me!

CARRIGALINE & ROBERT'S COVE

Training at the beginning of the season was a pleasure. We would go to Garrettstown and what a wonderful stretch of golden sand, and looking out at the Atlantic Ocean. Another place we would train at and one of my favourites was Robert's Cove. The five-a-sides on that beach were dynamite, and an old player used to join us, his name was Willie Cotter, who lived nearby in Carrigaline and was also a soccer reporter and journalist with the *Cork Examiner*. He used to join in the five-a-sides and was still a decent player at the age of 50.

Robert's Cove is a very unusual place. As you drive into it, one road only, there is the beach, the sea, and the cliffs on each side. And two old pubs called 'The Harbour Bar' and 'The Robert's Cove Inn.

It always reminds me of a scene out of Treasure Island and to sit outside having a drink and looking down at all this. Where else would you want to be? I would like to be down on that beach, playing football with the late Willie Cotter, and looking up and seeing an old bloke outside the pub, having a pint, reminding me about the life he had with a couple of other old codgers!

The last time I had a few drinks down there was in Rosies in Carrigaline, and what a good night it was. I went down with my pal Donal O'Flynn and we had made arrangements with Bobby Tambling and another pal whom I had played with for

Crosshaven, Buzz O'Connell.

By the end of the night, having had plenty of drink, I don't think we knew who we had played for! I know I left my car down there and went down with Donal to collect it, and it was still parked outside Rosies front door! So we agreed, we should have a pint, on the strength of the good night we had. There were only a few people in the bar. We ordered our drinks and were just chatting away and an old gentleman, reading his newspaper, looked over his glasses and said: "There was somebody famous in here with the same accent as yourself".

"What was his name", I asked, taking the mickey.

His reply was: "Fred Dibnah. He's the steeplejack, you know. The one off the telly from Bolton".

"Well, Donal, I think we better have two more pints after that, and another two after that".

ARTHUR, JEFF – CORK/KERRY

I lent my wife's car to a friend of mine, Jeff Partridge, and it was always in trouble, or the drivers were. He had been up to Montenotte, to the Country Club, with Keith Edwards, then the captain of Cork Celtic, and they had plenty of drink. They were stopped at the bottom of Summerhill by a Garda. This was the exact spot, and the same car, where I had been stopped months earlier when the Garda asked me to get out of the car and through the little driver's window, I said I could not do that, so he opened the door himself and the door came off its hinges, in one piece, and fell to the ground. I am still sitting there, and said, "That's why I could not get out".

Getting back to Jeff and Keith, they got off lightly. The Garda gave them a ticket and Jeff had to produce a driving licence and insurance. The mini was not insured by me or anybody else. Putting it mildly, it was a heap of shite and was ready for the knacker's yard. Jeff arrived at my house the following day and tells me what had gone on the night before. I said, "You're in trouble, but I will make a couple of phone calls and see what I can do."

I knew a lot of policemen and detectives in those days, but there were four very good friends of mine, Arthur, Bootsie and two of their pals, who I had some great times with, horse-racing, night clubs, magic lads they were. So off I went with Jeff into Cork to meet Arthur in the main police station on Union Quay (it's all moved to Anglesea Street these days)

In we go and ask for Arthur. He takes us up to his office, makes us a coffee and I have a cigar. He says, "Give me the docket", which has been issued to Jeff and then asked for a match. He burned it, in front of us. Our eyes popped out of our heads. Saved again! They were great days in Cork back then. I never had a tax disc on my car as they were all new ones I had bought in England and after twelve months the tax ran out and a Guinness label was displayed in the windscreen. It always served its purpose, but it did not seem to work when I went home to Bolton.

BOLTON'S SNOOKER BALLS !

I was with my pal Bally at Blackpool. He was then the Blackpool manager and lived there for a couple of years. Also it has a lot of memories for me as a child, as my Mum and Dad used to go there for our week's holiday in June. That week was officially Bolton Holiday week and everything closed down that week in the town.

You could not buy a loaf of bread as all the shops were closed. We would book the same boarding house (guest house) year in, year out. It was run by a lovely couple, Mr. and Mrs.

Spencer (no, not Frank!) and the same people were always there that week, for years on end. They were very happy times. My parents would take me to the famous tower, and to watch the circus, and see the most famous clown of all, the Italian Charlie Coroli. I was invited to a party at his house years later, but at 4.30am off he went fishing in his boat, as he did that every weekend.

Getting back to myself and Alan, we said we would have a walk along the promenade. It was a lovely afternoon. We were walking and chatting away, minding our own business, and on the beach in front of us a lady is absolutely banging the crap out of this gentleman. He looked very distressed.

"I think we should call a policeman", Alan said.

Just then, a policeman appears, pulls his truncheon out, and starts beating the man with it. That was the last straw. As we got closer, it was Punch and Judy! Gotcha

I had a lovely girlfriend in Bolton after moving back from Ireland. She was like an Arabian princess. Her name was Frances. I first met her in Valencia. We had been playing a European Cup game there years before and I was with a few players and my great friend, Billy George, who is also godfather to one of my sons. There she was, sitting in the same bar, where we had gone for a drink. I only said "Hello" and that was it until I was back in Bolton years later. We had some great times, but she drank a little too much. I remember being up at Tony Knowles's house in the Lake District. He had a snooker table in the house, as that's what he did for a living. He and his girlfriend had gone out for the evening, so we both stayed in and had a few drinks. We were mad in those days (still the same!) so we had sex on the snooker table, then started messing about. We had heard about the clitoris balls and both had a maximum break !

When Frances was living with me, which would never be more than a couple of months at a time, it was an electric combination. We had been out this particular night. We get in bed. She gets annoyed about something, jumps out of bed, puts on some clothes, and grabs her twenty-three inch television, which we used in the bedroom and marches downstairs with it. I am still in bed watching all this. I hear her ring a taxi downstairs and I go back to sleep. An hour later, I hear knocking on the front door, so I get up and go downstairs. I open the door. It's pouring rain and Frances is stood there, still with the big television beside her and soaked to the skin. She stood there, saying nothing. I said nothing. So I shut the door and went back to bed. A few weeks later, friends again, I ask her why did she knock on the door and say nothing and where was the taxi. She tells me the taxi came but when she picks the telly up off the ground outside the house, she walked towards the taxi but after two yards, the telly would not go any further as the plug at the end of the lead was stuck behind the front door. So when she knocked me up, and I got out of bed, when I opened the door, all she did was pull the plug out of the house. That's why she never spoke.

We're still friends today, and we laugh at the times we had together and have no regrets. I think it's nice when you can laugh at a strange relationship, which you had all those years ago, and we even joined the Mile High Club, on a trip to Lanzarote. Talk about no smoking in the toilets, it was just a hot oven, without smoke!

OFFICER'S MESS - COLLINS BARRACKS, CORK

I have a lot of great memories of Collins Barracks, the home of the Irish Army, and a credit to the country. I have met and made good friends with a lot of good people up there since 1969 to the present day, from majors and generals to corporals and privates ... all through the ranks. I took Cork Celtic up there one day back then to play a charity match for a soldier who had been hurt while on duty in Cyprus, and out there at that time was my old mate Joe O'Grady, who was also the Cork Hibernians goalkeeper.

An extrovert, to say the least, but he never let us down. In the warm-up before the match started, I would shoot a few balls at Joe to give him the 'feel' of the ball, then not being able to help myself, would blast a few into the back of the net. He would give me a look of disgust and I am sure he was thinking, after the game I will get my rifle and blow that English fucker to bits!

It was a few years ago, I got invited up to the Officer's Mess along with some pals from 96FM, Neil Prenderville, the late Frank O'Brien, Barry O'Mahony and Michael Ellard of the Irish Examiner. We all arrived for lunch. First we had drinks at the bar, and then taken into a beautifully laid out dining room, with just one long table. I was told where to sit by Commander Dave Harvey's staff and that was right next to himself. We had a delightful afternoon. The food was served to perfection, and so was the drink, and our host was great. I had an excellent conversation with him all afternoon. It was that good, we did not want to leave. When we did leave eventually, I borrowed the Commander's cap, walked to the door facing the parade ground, and a battalion of soldiers marched past.

I saluted them and they exchanged the gesture. We were all in uproar, in fact we all went back inside for another drink. What a day, and thanks again to Dave Harvey.

Two people whom I would like to pay my respects to, who were very good friends of mine were Captain Eamonn Young and Sargeant Paddy Drohan, who have both sadly passed away.

Eamonn was a very good squash player, whom I met through my pal Kieran Madden, who played tennis with me in tournaments in Rushbrooke and Paddy Tynan , I had known for a long time through the cricket fraternity.

The interesting conversations we used to have, over a quiet drink at the barracks, they were happy days.

I would like to say thank you to the Irish Army at Collins Barracks, and the fantastic job they do, and the work they don't get enough credit for. Signed: Corporal Davenport.

As I stated earlier, my Dad used to say that if you ever get behind that glass screen, meaning being on television, you will have done OK in life. I did do that by playing in televised matches, but I don't think he meant it in that way, that is collectively. He meant just me! I did that numerous times, with interviews with Trevor Welch, then with Neil Prenderville. It was a superb piece of interviewing, funny but they also covered a lot of exciting times in my life. A lot of people wrote into the *Evening Echo*, saying that it was one of the best interviews seen on television for a long time, which was nice to hear. I have some good friends at 96FM.

One of my pals, the late Frank O'Brien, helped me a lot and was always there for me, as is Donal O'Flynn. I am very lucky to have such good friends around me when I return to Cork. I have been very lucky ever since I arrived in Cork in 1967.

One such man, a top sports writer, Billy George, who worked for the *Cork Examiner*. He reported also on games we played in Europe, such as Valencia in Spain, and is also godfather to one of my sons. His favourite saying, which always amused me, is 'Keep the Faith', and he'd say it every time, instead of goodbye. I have known him for 40 years and more, and believe me, I still don't get it. Unless he meant that the old dressing rooms at Turner's Cross would not collapse on top of us, or there's always another one around the corner!

As I am getting towards the end of the book, I have just found out that I have become a granddad again for the third time by my daughter Samantha, and her name is Chyna. My other two grandchildren are both girls as well. Kyra and Teagan, who both live in America with my eldest son, Mark and his wife Carrie. My other son, Jason and wife Laura, are still trying and I need a boy to keep the Davenport name going, so come on lads, help me out!

I have a fantastic family and I am very lucky as divorces can make life very difficult. My ex-wife Jean and her partner Francis are great friends. I do regret missing out on my son's teenage years, as they were both good soccer players and played for their colleges in America.

I do believe if I had been around, they could have got on, with my coaching ability, to make it as professional footballers, as the eldest Mark, had an excellent left foot, and left peggers are hard to come by in the world of soccer. Most people outside the game would not realise that, but it's a fact.

It would have meant total dedication, hours of practice every day, no smoking, no drinking, no partying, no women. How the hell did I ever make the big-time! It was a miracle, a dream, or was it me?

As you get older, you start to appreciate things a lot more, like scenery, smells of nature, trees, the aroma of walking through woodlands, and sounds of the sea, and this gives you a quick flashback to your youth. I used to enjoy it when I was young and going for a Sunday picnic with my aunts and uncles, Mam and Dad, in three cars, each following the other into the countryside. They would find a nice, quiet spot in a woodland, get the chairs out of the boot, get the primus stove going, and all sit around having lunch. Why don't we start doing these things again? It's only making the effort. It keeps families together. If we don't show the younger generation, they will never know what they are missing. And if they don't want to come, make them. When I was about four or five, my aunties would ask me what I wanted to be when I got older. A footballer was my reply. Good for you, they would say with a smile.

I thought: "I will show you" and if every child has that determination in them, I am sure most would succeed, instead of making their minds up on the day they leave school. What happened thirty years ago, everybody wanted an office job or a job in the bank. Nobody wanted to be a tradesman, carpenter, plumber, plasterer.

In today's society, you cannot get hold of these people, as there is not a lot of them about, and if you do finally get hold of them, they can charge what they want.

Another thing about life, when you are over 50, people in the past used to save all their money. The way to go is to enjoy the time you have left in your life. Time is more precious than money, and so is good health.

Get your act together. Buy yourselves nice clothes, don't dress old-fashioned. Get in your car or on a plane. Do all the things you have ever dreamed of. You are only here the once!

MAJORIE PROOPS GETTING OLDER

As you get older, your body and mind don't work together like they used to. You take your time getting in and out of the bath. You forget what you went into the other room for. Did I leave the tap running? Was the appointment today or tomorrow? I can only remember two goals I scored, but cannot forget all the ladies!

I think the latter must have been more important! I will never forget the old gentleman who wrote to the Agony Aunt, Marjorie Proops, the letter went:

Dear Marjorie,

When I was 21, and I got an erection, I could not bend it, now I am 93 and when I get an erection, I can bend it. Do you think I am getting stronger?

Well, we all have our problems. You just have to get on with things. Viagra seems to be the in-thing at the moment. They say it stops you rolling out of bed!

I think the answer to that, take no tablets, just sleep in between two of the opposite sex!

Well, I have to go now. My carer has just arrived to put me to bed. She will tell me a story while I am finishing my Horlicks.

DECORATING BACK IN ENGLAND

When I returned from Cork back to Bolton, as well as playing football, I started a Painting and Decorating business, called 'Newlook', and it was very successful. I had numerous people working for me, one in particular was a lad called Philip. We were working on a job in Bolton, and every dinner time, I would send a pal of mine, Graham Hill, his father played with me at various times during my career, and also played for England. Graham would head off at 12.15pm and go to the pie shop, for our lunch. He would return with two meat and potato

147

pies each, but before we told Philip the pies had arrived, I would paint the bottoms of his pies with magnolia emulsion paint and with them being hot, they soon dried, and then we would shout to him and tell him dinner was ready. We would all sit down with our coffee and hand Philip his pies. After two weeks of doing this every dinner time and killing each other with laughter every day, I forgot to paint the pies. After he had eaten them both I said: "What do you think about the pies today, Philip?".

He replied, "Not as good as usual. Have they not come from the same shop?".

We never told him what we did.

On another job, there was a row of houses and we had to paint the outside windows and doors. It was No. 24 in the middle of the row. I was painting the front so I told Philip to start on the back of the house. When I went around to see how he was getting on and to tell him his pies were ready as it was lunch break, he was only painting the house next door !

When I told the lady who's house he had painted, she said: "Well, it needed doing and thank you very much".

On another occasion, I had come across gallons of green exterior paint, so every time I went to give an estimate for outside somebody's house, I used to say it would look great painted green, and would blend in well with the garden, and the surrounding trees. By the time I had got rid of that paint, half of Bolton was green, but it matched the environment. Nice one Dav!

PARTIALLY NAKED PARTY

I have had some strange experiences with women, without going into the gory details, you will just have to use your imagination.

Years ago in Bolton, I went to one of my pals' houses for his annual Christmas party and Terry Bolton always had a good one. This particular year was fancy dress. I decided I would go in a dinner suit, yes, always had strange choices in life!

It was a cold night. I put my overcoat on, got in the car and drove to the action. I could not wait to get there. Up the drive, park the car, knock on the front door and I go in. When I walk in all the guests are there, beautiful girls all in fancy dress, as are all my pals. I take my overcoat off and I look immaculate, from the front, but when I turn around, all the back of me is completely naked. I had cut the back out of all my clothes. It was hilarious to say the least. It was a fantastic party, but the best came later. At about 3am and everybody pretty intoxicated, the rest of my clothing was ripped off me, yes, starkers!

After a few more drinks, one of my lady friends asked if I could give her a lift home. "Oh yes", was my reply.

So we got in the car, she had not much clothing on, and me bollicks naked, and had to drive through the town centre of Bolton to get to where she lived.

But I had other things on my mind! We get to near her house and she suggests we stop on this piece of waste land about 300 yards from her house. I park the car and decide I wanted to release some fluid (a wee!). I get out and go behind some bushes. Next thing I hear the car starting up and she drives off, in the middle of winter. I am bollicks naked, no car, no clothes, and no money.

Could it get any worse? I don't think so, but what the hell, what can I do? I start looking in the dark for something to cover my privates but could not find a thing, except an empty rusted paint can, undercoat! It was an overcoat I needed!

I put the can over it, and held it there. It would have stayed there on its own, but it was too cold for that! My only solution was to walk to Jane's house, 300 yards away and I knew she lived with her parents. Oh my God! Her parents.

And it 4am in the morning and me with the paint can over dicky. I finally get to the house and my car is parked outside and it's locked. Only one option, Knock on the door and hope for the best. Door opens. Her dad in his pyjamas, my car keys in his hand. He says, with a smile, "Our Jane says thank you for the lift home and have a nice Christmas"!

LIFE & JOCK STRAP

I listen to a lot of men, and the talk of how many women they have slept with and I think, how sad is that? It's like trophy hunting. I have never spoken about it until now. Every one of the people I did that to, it was my pleasure and theirs too. It wasn't just for me. It was for them as well. It takes two to tango! I have always said when I went out with my pals after 9pm, no more talking about football as there were other more important things to look at and discuss, such as the opposite sex. But in the bar, up to 9 o'clock, with the lads, they could talk, tell jokes and that was great. But when the clock struck nine, it was every man for himself. Over the years, ever since I was sixteen, I have had magical times and experiences, beyond belief. Women together, three and four in a bed, no men, just me, so the clock soon went over two thousand, and it's still running. It's nothing I am proud of. And I definitely am not ashamed of it. That's the wonderful life I have had, and I am sure a lot of people would have liked to have been me, but I had the tools and the time. I am never going into any details, and never will, of my exploits, and would never lower myself to that level. My many friends who know me well, know I am a different person underneath than what I portray on the outside. I was asked what I thought about 'G' strings. I said I used to wear them thirty odd years ago. They were not out then. Oh they were, they were called Jock Straps! I once asked a question to some friends of mine. I asked who was the greatest holder of a ball to come down from Scotland to play in the English League. Various answers came up. Denis Law, Jim Baxter, Willie Johnstone, good choices I said, but no. The best one was Jock Strap. He has never lost one yet! Yes they were a marvellous invention as was the thing they were protecting, as none of us would be here today, but for him.

The Dav and big pal - Big Sam Allardyce, the ex-Limerick, Blackpool, Bolton, Newcastle, and now Blackburn Rovers boss enjoys an after-match drink in Sam's office at Ewood Park.

Frank Worthington(Leicester City, Bolton & England) with the Dav's mates Chris Posslewaithe and Jeff Partridge at Ian Greaves' (ex-Bolton Wanderers manager and Manchester Utd. player) funeral in Bolton.

BIG SAM'S BARGAIN BASEMENT

Managers come and go, you are only as good as your last game, that's an old saying in football, and that still holds in today's game. But most success today comes from not who is the best manager, but from which owner or chairman has the most money in the bank, and how much time they are prepared to give the manager to assemble new players, and get them playing together as a unit. A lot of my pals have managed Premier League clubs - Alan Ball, Southampton, Manchester City. Peter Reid, Manchester City, Sunderland. Sam Allardyce, Bolton Wanderers, Newcastle United and now Blackburn Rovers.

Take Sam as an example. He started his management career at Limerick in the second division in the League of Ireland. He was assistant manager at West Brom and Preston North End. Then got the Blackpool job, missed promotion after being league leaders, until the last two games. Then managed Notts County. Did a great job there as well. With a good record in management Sam gets his reward and becomes Bolton boss in 1999, a club with very little money.

He made signings which people would only dream of. Some on loan, others on 12 month contracts, but these players had been the best in the world at their peak, also World Cup heroes only a few years before.

How he got them to sign for Bolton is beyond belief. What a salesman. Alan Sugar eat your heart out. My boy's the best. Here is a list of his major signings:

Jay Jay Okocha, he was that good they named him twice. Nigerian captain, played in three World Cups.

Ivan Campo, Real Madrid & Spain.

Youri Djorkaeff, France. World Cup winner.

El-Hadji Diouf, African Player of the Year, three times.

Fernando Hierro, Real Madrid and Spain. Played in four World Cup tournaments.

Nicolas Anelka, Record signing, French international striker and has since been sold to Double champions, Chelsea for a profit !

Abdoulaye Faye - Sam took him to Newcastle for £3 million. A steal. Watch him! A great athlete!

There were a lot more good players brought in, but these were the back bone of a very good team, and the great thing was, they came mostly on free transfers, or for very little money, compared to other clubs.

Manchester United spent £87 million, and in the same season Bolton spent £6.5 million.

It was around this time that I wanted to start a new Cork team which was going to play at the home of Cork football, Turner's Cross.

All the financial side was in place and as we know from the past, two teams in Cork make money. You always have a game every weekend and the interest in the city is doubled.

I attended an FAI meeting in Dublin, along with my associates, the FAI Committee, a member of each League of Ireland club, and the Press. To cut a long story short, we did not get accepted into the league. Why they voted against me ? They were afraid of me getting success, as they had failed themselves in the past, and the main vote against me was from Cork City. I wonder why? And they did go back to Turner's Cross!

My plan for the new club was as follows, and would have won the league in my first season, with the players I had spoken to and through my proposed three year plan.

Looking back and even today, directors of football clubs don't have much knowledge about the game and never will. They like being in the papers or the T.V. It's most likely the only way they will get noticed in life, at least, they have a long career and never get the sack. So it looks O.K. Why have I never thought of being a manger?

Because I would not like to tell three people a year, that they're fired, and the whole country knowing I was an asshole! That reminds me. Getting back to Sam (chuckle). Great job at Bolton. In the final two for the England job. Would have done a better job than Steve McClaren - that's for sure! Why? Bigger personality and comes over with an air of confidence. But then chose Newcastle, a team of stars who cannot perform together. The ball's like a hot potato. They cannot wait to get rid of it. Before they receive it, they did not want it, crowd on your back, no confidence and your team in then a bad one, and to get that back, new players are needed, but these players must be winners and have big hearts. And most of all, don't like losing!

There are plenty of players who look great in training but cannot perform where it matters. And that's on the pitch with 50,000 people watching. For me, the bigger the crowd, the better I played. I wanted to show my skills and entertain them, and the more ball I got, the better I played. In fact, if they did not play to me, they would not be playing in the next game.

THE FINAL WHISTLE

As in every footballer's life, it's a very short career, I was very lucky. It lasted 20 years and I got paid to do something I loved. How lucky can you get? And all the friends you have made along the way. I would recommend it to any young lad, but he would have to be showing some skill around the age of eight, practice every day with the ball, and do not be side-tracked by others who are not dedicated to the career you want. And a big secret is eating healthy, plus fresh orange juice with two tablespoonfuls of pure honey in it, every morning of your life.

You will not go far wrong, as I never missed a morning since I was eight years old, and believe me, it's the finest tonic for your body in the world. When I look back over the past and a lot of my footballing friends who I had played with years ago, all died at a comparatively young age, and what a team they must have up there in Heaven now

Alex Ludzic, John Clifford, Tony Allen, Paul O'Donovan, Alan Ball, Paddy Shortt, John McCole, Dave Wigginton and George Best.

And when my contract runs out, it will be a great honour for me to play alongside them once again. I heard that they are top of the league, and the crowds are dying to get in! Good luck lads. You were magic to play with and were fantastic company.

As I have come to the end of my story, and things will never be the same again, I would not like them to be. We all have to move on and enjoy the rest of what's left. There's only one good thing about getting older, and that's everybody else is as well. Life has a lot of twists and turns, but you have got to make the most of the hand you have been dealt, and the big statement. It's never too late to change your life.

As for myself, I live in Spain for three months of the year now and what with time in Cork, Kinsale and Crosshaven, I am not in the U.K. as much these days.

I have a lot of friends in all three countries, so my life is pretty well organised at the moment. As for money, a Lottery win would not help, as I would be dead in six months and money has never been my God.

Give me a beautiful woman and a bag of chips any day!

As I have been writing this book, you will have read how many of my closest friends have passed away, and at a very young age, compared to the statistics of today's life span.

In past generations 50+ or 60 was considered old, but it is not by today's standards. We eat better, live better, have better health care, transplants etc. and we don't work as long or as hard. We are a very fortunate generation. But I don't think we appreciate it enough, and should look back to how our grandparents had to live hand to mouth.

I would just like to thank everybody connected with my Testimonial which took place a couple of years ago, against Bolton Wanderers and Cork City.

Big Sam who was then the manager, brought his full first team squad over and that included the fantastic J. J. Okocha and boy did he entertain the huge crowd that night. I was absolutely thrilled that the people of Cork came out in their thousands to support me. It brought back a lot of happy memories, especially, the game being played at Turner's Cross, the home of the first club I signed for, when I came across the water from England in the swinging 60s.

And that is over 40 years ago! And to get a crowd like that after all those years! I thank you and I am most humbled.

In the match programme, a lovely man called Gerry Desmond, wrote an article about me and also about that era in Cork and the match days on a Sunday. Even when I read that article today, it brings back all those great times I had in Cork and a tear or two, which shows the emotion and love I will always have for this great City, and when I visit it most definitely feels like where I belong. Home!

A day out at Mallow Golf Club.
Your may recognise a few of these!

Jimmy Barry Murphy (left) with Waterford's Alfie Hale
and former chairman of the Munster Senior League Jim Murphy.

Carl with Brian Barry Murphy at Bury's Gigg Lane ground after a night match.

Ex-Cork Celtic stars Pat O'Mahony and Ray Cowhie in jovial mood at
the Richie Brooks Night at the Evergreen Bar, Cork.

Cork Celtic's Donal Leahy and Cork Albert's & Cork Celtic 'keeper' Bertie O'Sullivan
at the Richie Brooks reunion at the Evergreen Bar, Cork.

REMEMBERING 'THE DAV'

In January 1967, Carl Davenport set foot in Turner's Cross for the first time. This evening he receives a belated Testimonial Match against Bolton Wanderers, his hometown club.

Gerry Desmond recalls the era when The Dav became a Leeside Legend.

He's a bit like Charles Mitchell, in a curious sort of way; if you're not of an age to easily recall the po-faced doyen of RTE news broadcasters shimmering across your black-and-white TV, most likely also you'll never even have heard of The Dav, let alone been lucky enough to see him play. Personalities of very different types, but sharing the same era of a now vanished Ireland, serious Charles used his Shakespearean timbre to convey shocking two-penny increases in the cost of bread to the nation, while effervescent Dav brought a riot of colour and a clatter of character to dull and boring Sunday afternoons. Ah, yes, Sunday afternoons in 1960s Ireland! You just had to be there, I guess, to appreciate everything that tedium can mean ...

Carl Davenport, who had been scoring goals for Macclesfield Town as if they were about to be removed from public usage, sailed into the unsuspecting, unprepared, sleepy southern capital in the middle of that slower-paced decade and signed for Cork Celtic. He must have wondered why, when he gathered his thoughts. Turner's Cross then, even through rose-tinted glasses, was an unkempt kip. Overgrown, unsheltered grassy banks on all sides with a ramshackle corrugated iron shed stapled together as a dressingroom, reeking of wintergreen. That season, 1966-67, was proving another mediocre one for Celtic who, despite a five-point improvement

161

on the previous year, would again finish second from bottom. Across the city, Cork Hibs clawed themselves up to one place higher, if only on goal difference. In all honesty, The Dav must have wondered why he had bothered. Mind you, he had done his bit immediately on the pitch, bagging nine goals to finish as the club's top striker in his first half season.

With a long catalogue of Murphys, O'Learys, McCarthys, Lynchs, Sullivans, Noonans and such, Corkonians were unlikely to spend their evenings supping pints and discussing the fancy-dan play of an English blow-in with a sissy name like Carl Davenport. He'd be ok, of course, in the modern era, as we're all Europeans now and everybody has funny names, but expecting 'Davenport' to trip regularly off tongues in Cork in 1967 was pushing things just a bit. And, to top it off, he had a girl's first name ... No, if he was going to be ours, he'd be The Dav, plain and simple like, well, like a decent pint of Murphs. Thus, The Dav was added to a litany of Leeside soccer nomenclatures: Brasso, The Golden Boy, Big Seanie, Small Seanie (see, we've got copyright on originality ...), Bunny, Bonty, Bootsie, Blondie, Four-Goal McCole, Chungum, Malla, Fadda ...

And ours The Dav became, riding the crest of a wave that belatedly brought a new professionalism to Cork football and tore it from the doldrums. The sea-change in Cork soccer was fuelled by the arrival of a flurry of other British imports such as Dave Wigginton, Dave Bacuzzi, Tony Marsden, John Lawson and Sonny Sweeney at Hibs, and Richie Brooks, Keith Edwards, Barry Notley, Alek Ludzik, Bobby Tambling and others at Celtic. Against a long tradition of English and Scottish mercenaries pitching their tents around sinking Cork clubs and then moving on, this group proved different: most of them either remained here after their playing careers were over, or held a deep affection for the city and those unmatchable times long after they had left. Almost without exception, the newcomers gradually worked their ways into the hearts of Hibs and Celtic fans. It was a mutual admiration society. The Dav himself, a frequent visitor to Cork, recalls it as 'The flower power era of football.'

Those late 60s early 70s years certainly had a feel-good factor about them on Leeside and in Waterford and Limerick too, while the game was all but washed up in Dublin at the time. There was a noticeable shift in the balance of power away from the capital. Waterford clocked up an incredible six league titles in eight seasons, Hibs and Celtic won championships, Limerick won the FAI Cup, Hibs claimed it twice while Blaxnit Cups, Shields, Dublin City Cups and Top Four Trophies were lifted with increasing frequency by the Munster clubs. Rivalries between the four were colossal, huge numbers attended games.

Through all of this, The Dav insinuated himself into Leeside folklore. He was immensely popular, even when he left Celtic to join Hibs, even when he left Hibs to return to Celtic. There were no 'Judas' taunts back then, despite the passion on the terraces and regular crowds of 12,000 or more. One derby match at the Cross, the year Celtic won the league, saw 18,000 shoe-horned into the place, and a similar number when they met in the 'Lodge later the same season. Interest peaked at the Hibs-Waterford title decider in 1972 when 26,000 crammed into the Lodge. Think about that, if we have a 'full house' of 7,000 this evening,

Crowds flocked to the Box and the Lodge in those days, of course, because Hibs and Celtic were successful or, at the very least, serious contenders for silverware. But they came also because they knew that they would be entertained, royally.

Those good times were great times, immeasurably so. There was less money about compared to today; we had no foreign holidays, few had cars and there was one television channel, mobile phones, CDs, DVDs, e-mail that stuff was science fiction.

It seems beyond imagination to me now almost, that characters as large a Davenport and Ludzik, for instance, could play for the same club, at the same time. Almost beyond belief. Either one was showman of sufficient skill, timing and savvy to be worth the admission alone for the amount of humour he could invest into a game, into any incident, as he saw fit. And they were skilful footballers as well, not just messers on the pitch, The Dav was a loveable rogue, and he knew it and milked it for all it was worth. And you knew that he knew it, and that made it even better somehow, Jeez, those were great days. We'll not see their like again, particularly as we are on course for full time football and the change in attitude that implies.

It would be wrong, however, to simply represent Alek or The Dav as comedians on a

football pitch. They appreciated the value of a laugh, for the crowd and for themselves for the game, if you like. We needed it: We lived in a grey, shuttered country. Although the times were a changing', they were still changin' a little too slowly for our generation. We needed something else, and The Dav, Wiggy , Alek & Co gave that to

us and then some. But they knew the serious. side of football also. They were artists and artisans, and they gave tremendous service to Cork soccer, however you care to gauge their contribution. They were champions too, let's not forget, and they wore that proud badge of achievement so valued by professionals with a swagger and a smile. The Dav, incidentally, is the only player among them to play in both

Hibs' arid Celtic's league winning sides.

This evening Bolton Wanderers, once famous as founder members of the Football League, later famous for the exploits of Nat Lofthouse, the Lion of Vienna, and now famous for being part of the juggernaut that is the Premiership, visit Turner's Cross. They are illustrious guests. Bolton, however, are here at Turner's Cross with a purpose: to pay tribute to a native son of the Lancashire town and a former player of the club, a man who lost his name on these shores but was adopted by the locals as The Dav. Tonight, then, sees the Carl Davenport Testimonial become a reality nearly three decades after he last togged out in that old corrugated dressingroom where the Club Shop and offices now stand.

The tragic recent losses of Wiggy and Alek, young men still, have taught us all to appreciate life a little more. Carl Davenport, with his goals and his laughter; enriched ours beyond measure at a time when we really needed it. Thankfully, he's still with us, despite a couple of scares, and we have an opportunity to show our appreciation. In Cork you still wear your Hibs or Celtic stripes, though the clubs have long ceased to exist, or you tell your buddies that your auld fella followed one or the other if the topic comes up in conversation. You may support Cork City now, but you'll always have Hibs or Celtic tucked away in your inside pocket. Pop into any bar in town, any night of the week and if you start a chat about League of Ireland football with anyone over 40, you'll be hearing tales of Alek and Wiggy before your pint is pulled. Before you know it The Dav will be recalled, and the stories will become even more colourful. The stories will be good ones: you'll not hear a bad word. And that in itself is a fitting testimonial to the man.

A curious thing happened on Leeside in the mid-to-late 70s.

Within a few years of their greatest successes, both Hibs and Celtic collapsed and, unforgivably, were allowed to disappear from Irish football. Their legacy was magnificent, but those left behind were bitter that their beloved clubs were lost to them forever. Many of that last Hibs and Celtic generation have retained that bitterness and have turned their backs on domestic football. They were lost to the game, like Hibs and Celtic themselves. They have their stories, their memories and their heroes from those halcyon days. I understand that: I was a Celtic fan, and I still am. But life, and football, goes on.

All those years ago, The Dav ran out week after week and stacked up a. lot of those memories for all of us, Hibs and Celts alike. We could all have left it there, at the back end of the 70's like a bunch of embittered Unionists harking for the way things were. Times change, c'est la vie, move. Carl Davenport was part of those days, those

unforgetable times, and he always will be.

He gave us a lot then, and he still can. He can be the catalyst for reclaiming some of that Lost Generation. Hopefully, they will be impressed by the changes in Turner's Cross; and impressed enough to return again to Cork matches and leave the bitterness behind, at last. Hopefully, we can heal some old wounds, keep the warm memories, the heroes of our teenage years gave us. We were a blessed generation: it is our own choosing if we decide to remain a cursed one by living in the past. If you never saw The Dav in action, it's unlikely that you will tonight, but you will see a genuine Leeside legend in the flesh nonetheless, one that deserves his big occasion. Turner's Cross was his stage, long before it was Dave Barry's or John O'Flynn's; this is his encore. Let's give him a big hand and let's enjoy it, like in the old days, which is how The Dav would want it.

Leeside Legends - the great Noel Murphy, one of Ireland's greatest rugby players and the Dav photographed at Cork Constitution RFC at Templehill.

Derry Looney, Miah Dennehy and John O'Neill - all played for St. Vincent's H&F Club as kids and remain the best of mates to this day.

Carl with best pal Paul Clements, former speedway and long track rider who competed against speedway greats such as Peter Collins, Ivan Mauger and Bruce Penhall at the famous 'Stone of Accord' at The Old Head Golf Club, Kinsale

SAT NAV DAV AND THE SONG

Many thanks to the people who have helped me along the way to get this book published - Barry O'Mahony and the late Frank O'Brien of 96 FM, Alice De la Cour of the Irish Examiner, Noel Spillane and John Roycroft of the Evening Echo, also to John O'Neill who wrote and sang 'Sat Nav Dav,' which is bubbling under in the charts.

All the proceeds of the CD are going to the Meningitis Research Foundation. The song is about when I came to Cork in January 1967, there were only 200 people at the 'Cross and the same at Flower Lodge. The season after there were 20,000 at the games and I settled by the banks of the Lee, my digs were on the Mardyke, my old mate and trainer Timmy Murphy (Beckett), Billy Morgan, Jimmy Barry Murphy , Jack Lynch and 'Ringy' from the Glen, all greats at their individual sports

John then does a football commentary in between the great Irish music and fiddle playing and mentions all my pals who I have played with over the years who have regrettably passed away. Alan Ball, George Best, Paddy Shortt. There is also a tribute to Cork Celtic and Cork Hibernians players of my era, and they can hold their heads up high as they were the best, and always will be, there will never be two teams like them again.

History will prove that.

96FM & THE INCOME TAX

I was staying with my pal Jim Good in Kinsale and we had been out a bit late this particular night, so off we went to bed .. not together mind as I am still in the cupboard at this stage .. Ha, ha.

The following morning about 9.30a.m Jim comes into my room and says: "Get up you bugger, you have a 'phone call."

I get out of bed feeling a bit rough, go downstairs and take the call.

This voice says: "Mr. Davenport I am from the Inspector of Taxes"

My reply: "Oh yes.

"It has come to light that since 1967 to 1975 you were playing for the Cork clubs – Celtic and Hibernians and you were getting wages of around £180 a week.

And you never paid a single penny tax.

My reply: "Oh" and then he says with all the interest that has accumulated over the years you owe us £17,500 and we want to know what are you going to do about it ?

You have been seen driving around Kinsale in your fancy car and smoking a big cigar.

Reply: "Oh."

He then says would I come over to the tax office on the South Mall .. Room 220 on the third floor and discuss the matter of repayments or would he come down to Kinsale to meet me tomorrow.

"Don't bother," was my response "because in one hour's time I will be on the fastest boat out of Kinsale harbour and you will never see me again. It will be full speed ahead.

Oh you can have the car !

He then starts laughing and says:"This is Mick Mulcahy and we are 'live' on 96FM and this has been a wind-up.

Talk about shit....g yourself ….. he had set it all up the day before with Jim !

FRANK O'BRIEN RIP

To end this book which has taken me about four years to finish, which is totally unprintable, but that's me, and a lot of things have happened since.

My pal and great friend Frank O'Brien passed away suddenly, and I was shocked and saddened, as I was with him only two weeks before, he was a fun guy.

I remember doing a commentary with him at Turner's Cross, Cork City v St. Patricks Athletic, it was a cold day, the game was not very exciting, it was a radio commentary, and we were in the Press Box. Frank was talking away and said I will hand you over to 'the Dav' who is sitting next to me. Thanks Frank, Yes, it's a very open game, not many shots on goal, I think one goal will win it, by either side. Thanks, Dav. He then said which was the best club I played for? My reply was 'The Carousal', which was a notorious night club in the old days that I used to frequent.

Well he started to laugh and people started to ring into the radio station, it was hilarious, thanks Frank for the fantastic memories and I will truly miss you.

It will never be the same again.

HEART ATTACKS - LIFE SOON PASSES YOU BY

Life soon passes you by, and the older you get, time seems to go very quickly, and as soccer players, well as you look back, it's just like the blink of an eye, I played for twenty years as a professional that was my job, which I got paid for, and I enjoyed every minute of it. Would I have done it differently if I had my life over again? No!

When I saw old players who had played years before me, and they would be my age now, I had respect for them but could not picture them training around a soccer pitch, defending or scoring goals, or in a dance hall chatting the ladies up, but now I am one of those old ex-professional footballers, and the players of today will be thinking exactly as I thought all those years ago. How could that old sod, have been any good, bet he never had all those ladies, he was supposed to have had. He could not run to catch a bus. Now I could if it were stopped.

Up to the age of 52, I trained three mornings a week in a park in Bolton, doing exercises, jogging and twenty yard sprints, all on grass, no roadwork, which is very bad for your legs, even if you are a young person. I kept myself fit. No I was not thinking of playing again, it was for my self-esteem, to feel good, keeping my body in shape and to live longer. Yes, it worked, until about four years later; I met a lovely lady about ten years younger than myself, and fell in love.

It was perfect for a year until I found out she had a drink problem, which continued to get worse over the years, I used to hate the sound of a can of lager opening at 10.00 am in the morning, that noise from the can, it was like someone shoving a knife into me and this went on all day and night. If we went on holiday abroad and went to the beach, the sun boiling down at 90 degrees she would bring with her a six pack of Stella lagers, people would look at us, it was embarrassing to say the least. I stuck the drinking and abuse for four years as it got to a stage she never went out of her house, just drank solidly all day until she was out of drink or collapsed into bed. So I decided to end the relationship, having tried everything from Alcoholics Anonymous to hospital treatments. Nobody could have tried harder and the support I gave her, but for once in my life this problem beat me, and nearly killed me!

By now I am living back at home, and that's about two miles away from the lady in question. I get a phone call about 11.30 am, could you come to my house, I am very ill and need help quickly, I said I would, but would be a half an hour, as my car was in for a service. I set off from my house running and walking, sweat pouring off me and stressed out, I arrive, she was not ill, but drunk as a skunk, the house looked like a bomb had hit it. Well, before I could say or do anything, she started balling and shouting abuse at me, this got me worked up, and it developed into a shouting match. I went outside the house for some air, while outside I felt faint and weak, I managed to get back indoors and onto the settee, but feeling my life was over, managed to dial 999, and an ambulance came within minutes, Thank God.

On arrival the two medics put me on a stretcher, along with an oxygen mask on my face, and into the ambulance. My thoughts on the way to the hospital, which was only three miles away, will they make it in time or will it be too late. It was the longest three miles I have ever had to travel, and the noise and the sirens, to get the traffic to move out of the way, I never before thought about the poor bugger in the back, whose life depended on it, I do now!.

When the ambulance arrived at the hospital, that was one bonus for me, and only a few more yards to go before I was put on a table and doctors were around me, asking me questions, the last one being will you have this injection, but we have to have your permission, "Why, was my reply?" "It can go wrong" that's all I needed, "What's the percentage?" I asked, 80%, that seemed good enough odds for me, carry on then, was my answer.

At that stage and near to deaths door, I would have taken a chance on anything they had to offer. I lay there for about three hours and started to feel better, the specialist came back and asked me how I was, I said, fine, is it Ok for me to go home. He looked at me, smiled, you're joking, you're off to the intensive care unit, and off on the trolley I went, and remained there, wired up to more machines, than they have to run the illuminations at Blackpool and there I remained for three weeks.

When it came to the time that I was being readied for discharge from hospital, it was strange, but, I did not want to go home. I felt safe there, and all the doctors and nurses at the Bolton General Hospital, had been fantastic to me and I could not praise them enough. No wonder, I always donate to the Heart Foundation. I would give a lot more if I was wealthier, but better still, I'm alive, and how much is that worth!

The lovely lady in question, and the cause of my attack, does not touch a drop any more having nearly killed herself and me. She has changed her life around, thank God, she is a new person, her house is immaculate, she looks a Million Dollars, using her car again, having not driven for four years, as she was unable. It's a new beginning for her, a new life, so all my efforts over the years have eventually paid off and we are still good friends but it's still hard to get my head around it as she is totally different in everyway, and I am so pleased for her after a life of alcoholism. Now she can enjoy and see the things she missed out on, for all those years, it will be like having new lenses in your glasses.

When I arrived home from hospital, I felt very tired, and did not feel well, also very afraid of having another attack. The doctors had told me to do a lot of walking. Six weeks went by and was due for my check up. Off I went for my appointment at 11.00 am. I am still feeling terrible, I said to the doc. He examined me. I told him how I had been during the past six weeks, he then says, I want you to get on the walking machine, I am all wired up with wires everywhere. He switches it on, but, me like an idiot, wishing to prove to him, that there was still life in the old dog yet, I stayed on for seven minutes, but I was knackered. You have done well, he says, and off I went home still feeling unwell. I wake up the following morning, make myself a cup of coffee, and sit on the sofa, felt weak, grasping for breath, and thinking this is goodbye. I managed to telephone 999 and the ambulance is on the way. Yes, another Heart Attack, and back in hospital again for another three weeks at least. I knew everybody by this time, and I used to put together quizzes for people in the same ward. One day we had a quiz on 'Heartbeat' that's the show on the TV. That made them smile. What happened to me, to bring on the second attack, I still had a small blockage in an artery which had gone unnoticed and when I went on the walking machine, the blood could not circulate past it. I suppose it is like a car, when the petrol can't get through to the engine. I am alive to tell the tale, but it took me 18 months to get myself fit and well. Now I take tablets daily and look forward to taking them as a lot of people never get the chance, some people get a Heart Attack and they're gone. That has happened to a lot of my friends, and at times I feel that I have cheated death, I am still alive, and they never get another chance. I learned one thing from it, appreciate life more, don't worry about things, and make sure you do what you want, in the time you have, and more importantly. enjoy every minute of every day, as your house, the money you have in the Bank will be there after you've gone. Be intelligent for once, start to live and worry about nothing.

My father-in-law, George Crosbie, passed away a few months back aged 84; George was an active man all his life. He and his family ran the Cork (now) "Irish Examiner" as well as the evening paper "Evening Echo." George was a keen golfer and played for Ireland alongside such greats as Joe Carr, Jimmy Bruen and others and he was also a keen sailor, being a member of the Kinsale Yacht Club and the Royal Cork Yacht Club, the world's oldest and founded in 1720 !

He was also non-playing captain of the Irish amateur team which won a European trophy.

When the family lived in Cork, they had a large house in Douglas, which they needed as Joan, George's lovely wife had given birth to eight children, and as it was only around the corner from Flower Lodge, the home of Cork Hibernians, George would bring his young son, Paul, to watch me play.

George thanks for the memories; even though my marriage only lasted five years, we remained good friends until the day he died. He always said: "You should still be my son-in-law, my reply being: " George, we will leave it on that note," and we just laughed.

Cheers George.

Carl on a courtesy visit to the then Lord Mayor of Cork, John Maloney at The City Hall.
Also included in the snap are - back row left to right -
Austin Noonan, John Coughlan, Donie Leahy and Pat Goggin
Front row from left - The Lord Mayor, Carl Davenport and the late Frank O'Brien of 96fm fame.

"It was like ... Cork Celtic legend Donie Leahy makes a point to Echo columnist
and Cork soccer historian Plunkett Carter."

REFLEXO - NEW TRAINING METHOD

When I was over in Cork last, I was introduced by a friend of mine Noel Spillane, a journalist with the Evening Echo, to a lovely man, John Joe O'Sullivan, who has invented a new computerised device called REFLEX O. He took me down to Little Island, just outside Cork City, to have a look at it, and I was quite surprised. It had one set of full sized goal posts and a machine in the middle that fired out footballs at different angles and different speeds, a light would also flash to tell the players facing the goal at which direction the ball was coming from.

The machine - a coaching aid - can hold and fire out balls at short intervals, so the player is kept moving and kept on his toes, firing them back into the net as randomly as they come at him, after ten minutes of shooting practice, he's shattered.

I was impressed so much, I asked my pal Sam Allardyce at Blackburn Rovers if John Joe could bring it over and let them have a look at it, which he did, and set it up in the indoor arena, which is a huge place with fantastic astro-turf and as large as half a soccer pitch. The coaches and the technical staff were very impressed, and after trying it out each coach was put through a period of ten minutes each, they were on their knees after the session is videoed by a hidden camera and the manager or coach can watch them on screen while they are in their office. This project could be of benefit to clubs around the world and ideal for the young lads coming through their academies. Yet another great innovation to come out of Cork City. Well done John Joe, incidentally John Joe played his football with Rockmount under the guidance of Denis O'Donovan.

THE REST OF MY DAYS

I have been giving a lot of thought about the rest of my life, such questions as, how long have I got left before they screw down the lid? I expect we all would have that feeling at sometime or other, but really we don't want to know. My plan is to stay healthy if possible, plan more things for the weeks and months ahead and cherish every minute as nobody lives for ever. My Dad used to say, there is only one thing good about getting old, and that's everybody else is getting old with you, how true, so there's food for thought in that statement.

Another thing he said was I don't like salad, why Dad? Because is grows to near the ground, think about that one?

Well I have decided what road I am going to take and it is a big road, a luxury Camper Van, and the four walls of my house. They will still be there when I have departed from this planet. I will select a country where the weather will be good, switch the "Sat Nav Dav" on and I am away for a couple of months, but will always return to the Green Green Grass of Home in the summer. And anyone wishing to join me can apply by e-mail to dav.com. I will do the cooking. What would be nicer than a trip to Galway on Race Week, then south to Bantry Bay, Schull, Timoleague and on to Kinsale.

That trip would be as good as it gets, even if you travelled the world, you would not find scenery like it, or get the stories over a pint of Guinness with the locals at each stop you make. Bring it on. I can't wait. Buntus Cainte, it is something like that, you know what I mean?

STAR PLAYERS IN IRELAND

If you go back to the late sixties, early seventies, most teams in the League of Ireland had star players, who could have performed in the English Leagues. Johnny Fulham played in the Preston North End team, when they were in the old English First Division (now the Premiership), and played alongside the likes of the great Tom Finney. I was also playing for them at that time, Johnny went missing during the season, and it was reported that he had got homesick and had returned to Ireland, to his beloved Dublin, where he joined the great Shamrock Rovers and played for them as an outstanding wing half for many years, in fact when I came to Ireland in 1967, I played against him on many subsequent occasions for Cork Hibernians and Cork Celtic. Rovers had many great players but one in particular Frank O'Neill, an outside right, who I would say was the best player of all time, in that position to play in League of Ireland. Another good friend of mine John Keogh, played in the same team, at right full back, in later years I signed John, when I was in charge at Cork Celtic, and with his experience he did a great job for me. He still lives in Dublin and had a furniture business as well as a guest house with his lovely wife, Eileen. I stay there when I am in Dublin, and we chat about the old times we had and the enjoyment we got from the game. We were lucky; we would not get that today, no stories, no drinking, and no mixing with the public, just a big house on the hill, your wife and the dog. Give me the old terraced house, good neighbours, kids playing with other kids, going to the cinema, and family holidays in Blackpool or Torquay and in those days, there was nobody on the team who could not speak English, or did not know what a pie or a steak pudding looked like.

I remember one game at Flower Lodge, a friend of mine was sitting in the stand, and I had shot over the bar, and someone in the crowd shouted in a loud voice " Dav you would not score in a brothel, there was quietness and a voice said: "I bet he would!

YOUGHAL

Youghal was always a favourite place of mine, it had plenty of attractions, a dance hall called, Red Barn, where thousands of people from Cork, would travel down there every weekend. Perks Amusements, Sir Walter Raleigh Hotel, The great film Moby Dick, starring Gregory Peck was shot there. When I was in digs on the Mardyke, a lad called John Doyle, a student at the University, very clever student, I think he was studying Engineering, also stayed in the digs. We spent a lot of free time together, especially with the ladies.

John's parents had a shop on the left hand side of the main street in Youghal on the way to Waterford. It was just called 'Doyles.' I think it was a hardware shop, just like that of my parents shop in England. My first girl friend was also from Youghal, a lovely girl who I met at a dance in Red Barn one summer. Her name was Cora Stack. She also lived in the Main Street, I was very fond of Cora. I remember she had a brother, a priest, I met him on numerous occasions, a very nice man. A couple of years ago, I was on my way up to Waterford and I heard that Cora had worked for a Solicitor, I called in to see her, but she was off for the day. It's a very quaint old fishing town with nice beaches. If you take the coast road from Cork to Dublin. That's the first place you pass through, but the scenery on the way up, has to be seen to be believed.

PATSY DORGAN

This poem was written by a lovely man, who I met many times. His name is Patsy Dorgan. He worked at Cork Airport for 32 years, and as a young man played for Blackburn Rovers, a team who I go and watch all their home games as my pal Sam Allerdyce (Big Sam) is now manager there. Patsy also played with Cork Hibernians, before my time, sorry Patsy. He also attended, St. Joseph's School in the Mardyke, and that's the area where I lived when I first came over from England. Also I played cricket for Wanderers with Patsy's friend Pat Dineen, up the 'Dyke. Patsy has just had a book published, a beautiful read, on poems, which he has written himself.

When I read all the poems, I had a tear in my eye, they were so pure and from the heart of a true Cork man, but, one especially took my fancy, it's called "My Old Man". I have put this into my book in memory of my dad, and if you have a Dad, you will like it too. Thank you Patsy, that's fantastic.

All the proceeds of these poems are going to the Irish Cancer Society.

MY OLD MAN

My thoughts are often of you,
And the happy times we shared.
In my success and failures,
You always showed you cared.
So well I can remember,
Whenever I felt sad.
You were the one I turned to,
The greatest, one could have

You watched me in those moments,
When I could not last the course.
And your kind words and wisdom,
Led me to a better source.
Often Mum would chide you,
How soft you used to be.
She knew so well your gentleness,
And loved you, just like me.

Now that I have grown up,
A life to call my own.
I cherish still the memories,
And all that you have shown.
You've been my guiding influence,
In what I do and say.
A reason for the blessing,
That I enjoy today.

If only I could see you more,
But land and sea divide,
Yet, thoughts that fill the heart,
Keep you constant, at my side.
Time can not erase the feelings,
Enshrined, since life began.
Neither shall it falter,
In the love for my "Old Man"

Carl gets an earful from his pal, Johno on guitar in his recording studio
in the Derbyshire hills in the Spring of 2009

Look at it now! The Dav back at the 28,000 all-seater Reebok Stadium in Bolton
.... back where it all kicked-off '"well not quite!
Carl started his career at Burnden Park in 1959.

BIRTH OF MY DAUGHTER, SAMANTHA

I had been back in Bolton for four years since leaving Cork, and was playing for Radcliffe Borough, a non league team, just about twenty minutes from where I lived. My pal and I, alias, Freddie Hill, who played for Bolton Wanderers, the same time as I did, and who also had played for his country at International level. Our Manager, Ken Wright, had good knowledge of the standard of football that was played at this level. I remember at one training session, it was a Thursday night and behind the clubhouse was a small piece of land with just one light on the side of the wall, to train under. Myself and Fred were dictating the pace of the running, the rest of the lads, behind us, clever that, all at once the one light went out, we were in pitch darkness. I shout over to the club house, the window being open, as the cable for the one light went through there, into the plug on the wall. I shout, "Put that fucking light back on" a voice shouts back at me, sorry mate, there's a pool match just starting, there's only one plug. My reply, I hope you win.

Another time after training, we had not been at the club that long, and we were at the end of our careers, we must have looked old to the rest of the players, average age must have been about nineteen and one young lad said to Fred, "What was your last club", Fred said: "Oh, England, I started laughing but I don't think they got it. When we played home games and we won, one of the supporters would put a bottle of Johnny Walker Whisky on the bar for the team after the game. And the strange thing was, lucky enough the rest of the them did not drink. We loved home games.

After one particular home game, yes, we had won again, into the bar we went, it was a very large room, where a lot of functions, and top class artists would perform, such as Cannon and Ball, the Bachelors, and many more, they also had a resident organist, who did the backing for most acts, a good looking lady called Denise with an excellent body and she was only seventeen. Well it did not take me long to make a move, so I sent her a drink, and that was the start of yet another relationship. After a couple of months we decided we would live together, at the time I had bought a new car, a Yellow TR7 Sports, one of the first in Bolton. You would press a switch and the headlights would come up. I thought it was great, Oh easily amused. So then I decided to buy a four berth caravan and go down the south of England to Torquay, yes, I always had fond memories down there, through my parents and aunties and uncles taking me there when I was a child. So not being a travelling wilberry (good on you Roy) how do I get the caravan down to Torquay. Easy, I go and get a tow-bar and got it fixed onto the TR7, you're right, it was the only tow-bar ever fixed to a sports car. We then packed the caravan with everything we needed, and off up the road we go. After 20 yards, I look through the rear view mirror and the caravan has come loose, and off on its own down the hill, but for my friends who had been waving us off, it could have caused havoc or even killed someone. We fixed the tow-bar on again, properly this time, but it thought me a big lesson, check things more carefully in the future.

We did reach Torquay eventually, and found a lovely site near Tiverton, which is beautiful countryside with very friendly people. A couple of weeks passed and I met a lovely man, John, and he was involved with a local football club, and asked me if I would coach them, and help them progress. They had a beautiful pitch and class changing rooms. That's all you need to start a team. I told him what I needed for my first training session, a whistle, poles and footballs, and we were up and running. The players enjoyed every minute of it and that's what's important, after about six weeks I had got them fit, and playing to a formation that would suit them. It was time now for Denise and I to return to Bolton, saying our farewells to the many friends we had met down there. One of the special things that happened while down there, Denise got pregnant, and so my beautiful daughter, Samantha was born. She's 32 now with two daughter of her own, called Chyna and Lola, it's like the song "what Lola wants, Lola gets."

As for Tiverton FC, I believe they got a proper all-seater ground, and are not many divisions off the Football League. Like my Dad used to say: "You've got to start somewhere."

Carl with great pal Franny Lee at his home in Wimslow, Cheshire

Carl and his then wife Jean (Crosbie) pictured with their first born son Mark in Blackrock, Cork in 1971 with the Dav's proud parents Jim and Hilda

Pointing the way ...
Carl back at his old stomping ground Flower Lodge with his son Jason

Carl back at Flower Lodge or should that be Pairc Ui Rinn having been granted permission by the Cork County Board to do a photo-shoot there.

Family Portrait: The Dav's children - Mark, Samantha & Jason - pictured in Kinsale, Co. Cork in the summer of 2000

CORK CENTRE FORWARDS

THROUGH the years there have been some great scoring centre forwards, who could win games when the going got tough. They had natural ability on the ball, and most importantly had an eye for goal. I was lucky enough to play with two of them, Austin Noonan was one, and that was when I signed for Cork Hibernians from Cork Celtic in 1970. Austin was in his twilight years, so he did not play many games, but he was a player with a great footballing brain, who could score goals, but most importantly, he could hold the ball up, with his close control, and bringing other players into the game. Two years later he took over as manager of Hibs, after the sacking of Amby Fogarty, another big mistake. Austin took over the reins and made an immediate impact as manager. In his day, if he had been left in charge of Cork Hibernians, we would have won the league for the next couple of seasons and every other trophy as well. Also Cork Hibernians would probably be still in business too and still at Flower Lodge

Dave Bacuzzi was a man who had an ego trip, not for the team, but for himself. He did not like me, why? Well, here are the facts. At first I used to babysit for him and his wife in Douglas. I was courting Jean Crosbie at the time, whom I married later, but when I got married, he did not like it, as Jean's parents, were the owners of the Cork Examiner, and it was, which he thought a step above him. Also two years before he arrived, I had been bought by Amby Fogarty for a record fee, from neighbours Cork Celtic. Also I was on £180 per week, he was most likely on less, but I was one of the players who the rest of the lads looked up to and a great bunch they were to, from Joe Grady, Frankie Connolly, Martin Sheehan, Noel O'Mahony, John Herrick, John Lawson, great left peg, Sonny Sweeney, fitness fanatic (if you lost your dog he would keep going until he found it), Miah Dennehy, Tony Marsden, 'Wiggy' and Terry Young, who was in the Army and an excellent left-winger, tricky, but was very fast and direct, and crossed a great ball. He was not always available for selection, so this position was shared with Donie Wallace, who was coming to the end of his career, but was still very effective, but lacked the pace of Terry Young. To return to Mr. Bacuzzi, he must have felt inferior in his mind as he was only a right full back, and as I have said before, the man he replaced in that position was Frankie Connolly, a better player, by far. Frankie used to play on the right wing, as he had skill, speed and intelligence, so when he moved to full back it was easy for him, and he ended up, as one of the best right backs in Ireland, until Bacuzzi arrived: "Your in my position, your fired! As in the Apprentice. As for myself, he would make me do extra training, I think he tried to kill me off. It was like being in a concentration camp. It did not matter to him, how well I was playing, or how many goals I was scoring, he tried to break me, as they say in prison. That's only what I have heard, but that's the way it was, it would have been better in Shawshank.

My two pals, Wiggy and John Lawson they knew what he was doing to me, we used to joke about it, but I never gave in to him, as I was too good of a player, twenty times better than he ever was, and that is a fact.

A host of clubs wanted to sign me around that time, English as well as the top Irish teams, but I was not going to be made to move from my beloved city of Cork. It was my home. Around two years later Dave Bacuzzi did leave Cork, after he had run the club into the ground, and into extinction.

I have heard since that, he had no regrets, well I have, I had gone from the club two years before this happened, and signed again for Cork Celtic, under manager, Paul O'Donovan and went on that season to win the league title, this was my third time and last time. I played for Cork Celtic and I loved Turner's Cross, as that was where my time in Ireland started.

DONIE LEAHY

Another old fashioned centre forward, which every team should have, even in today's teams, was Donie Leahy. A great friend of mine, and was one of the first people I met when I arrived in Cork. He and his lovely wife, Pauline, would invite me up to their house for a meal, the night before a game to keep me out of trouble. I would think, Donie was a great leader, but his main strength was holding the ball, with his back to goal, and laying it off to his support players, like myself. I used him at centre-half, if we had injuries, but that was easy for him, years later he moved to and played for Limerick, along with his brother-in-law, Paddy Shortt, who I had introduced into League of Ireland soccer years before. When I managed Celtic, for the first time they were both very successful with Limerick and put the club back into the spotlight once again, after being in the doldrums for a few seasons.

A TRIBUTE TO CORK HIBS

1.

In Cork we have a Soccer Team who play in Green and White.
We call them Cork Hibernians, to watch them is delight.
A style they have perfected, they call it push and run
And it's brought back the League to Cork, the first since Fifty One.
Chorus: They're Football crazy, they're Football mad,
     They're the League of Ireland Champions
     Bacuzzi's super squad.

2.

In goal we've got Joe Grady, who's over six feet tall,
He's fronted by John Herrick, who's always on the ball
You can't let out Frank Connolly, or Bacuzzi who's the boss,
Not forgetting Noel O'Mahony who hails from Turner's Cross.

Chorus

3.

Now at mid field we've got two Scots, who come from Glasgow
Town,
There's fair haired Sonny Sweeney, who covers lots of ground,
Longside him Johnny Lawson whose shot packs quite a sting
And Bolton's Carl Davenport, the man we call the king.
Chorus

4.

Up front we've got Dave Wigginton, of Derby County fame
And new boy Tony Marsden, who's scored a goal a game.
Who can forget young Dennehy, and Donie Wallace too
Who's famed for skill and sportsmanship, his equals they are few.
Chorus

5.

Now for reserves we have stars too, as strange as this may seem
There's singing star Liam Dennehy, who'd walk in to any team.
There's Chapman, Young and Finnegan O'Donovan and Field.
When called they did their bit for Hibs, an inch they did not yield.
Chorus

6.
Now every team in Ireland to knock us is their aim,
Some will even adopt tactics which are not within the game.
But every time we play them the story's as before.
They may have got one goal, but it's Cork Hibs three or four.
Chorus
7.
Now that's the story of Cork Hibs, a name that is widespread
The mention of this glorious name fill other teams with dread
So step forward Dave Bacuzzi to receive your wide acclaim
To every team in Ireland now, you're more than just a name.

Verses composed by Mrs. Bernie O'Sullivan and given to me by a
singer-song writer Oliver O'Regan from Kinsale – a good friend of
mine.

MY LIFE TODAY

Well the book is finished now, I must have had a boring life, as
I can't find much more to write about. The memory is not as
good, and I can't tell you everything. But one thing for certain,
I can tell a bad team, when I see one, when I saw Newcastle's
first game last season, at home to Wigan Athletic, Newcastle
won 1 – 0, but I said earlier in the book, they would be
relegated and they were.

 I go to watch Bolton and Blackburn when I can, and I hope
they can survive another season in the Premiership, as neither
club has the funds to buy top players, but luckily enough,
there's many more in the same boat.

I am a member of the former Player's Association at both
Bolton and Preston North End and both clubs have an itinerary
of events which are planned for each year such as Golf days,
Cricket Matches and Bowling (Crown green – not the Irish
Road Bowling) tournaments against other soccer clubs, and its

great to meet players of the past, of your own era, and socialise with them and discuss old times. We see a lot of the ex-Wigan players, they are a great bunch of lads, and our Bowling competitions are home and away. We have a trophy which we play for and it's precious stuff but so is the drinking afterwards.

My old pal, Dickie Arnold, plays for them, but as young lads we both started our football careers at Bolton Wanderers. Dickie was a right winger, slim fast and tricky, at that time my other mate Francis Lee, was fighting for the same position, and Francis went on to be a regular international for his country. I had not seen Dickie for forty years, since we were at Bolton, yes, he had changed, he was not that little ferret that went down that wing at speed, and I was not the fellow who banged goals in every week. TOUCHE.

The Dav with ex-Cork City and Glasgow Celtic midfield star, Mick Conroy and the Evening Echo's soccer correspondent Noel Spillane at The Clarion Hotel, Cork.

NOEL SPILLANE interviews some of the Dav's old team-mates and opponents.

NOEL O'MAHONY:

Noel O'Mahony was captain of Cork Hibernians for four years at the height of their prowess. To Noel the captaincy was far more than just going up to the centre-circle to meet the ref and toss a coin to decide ends. Noel was an excellent skipper and in that period he says that he had no big issues with 'the Dav'.

"Carl was a very good professional and he never caused me any bother when I was skipper and in charge of the team. He scored lots of goals and great goals ... and he always had an eye for goal. When I look back on it, it was a privilege to play with Carl and Dave Wigginton in the same team. We had two of the best strikers in the league at that time and they were two exceptional players," said Noel, who admitted to being disappointed with the Dav when he jumped ship and moved to bitter city rivals Cork Celtic. "I was disappointed when he left Hibs for Cork Celtic because I felt he was always going to be good for Cork Hibs anyway. But he was allowed go and that upset me as team captain. Tony Marsden came in as a replacement so it was player for player at that stage and the Dav moved on. It was a shame but that was football then and it's the exact same today," said Noel who also played against the Dav when he was at Turner's Cross.

"Carl was a unique talent in many ways as a person and as a footballer. He won league medals with Cork Hibs and with Cork Celtic in the space of three years and not too many fellows did that here."

O'Mahony who won the inaugural Cork Schoolboys League "Player of the Year" award in 1958 and started his League of

Ireland career in 1961 after spells at Ballyphehane United and Tramore Athletic, said that Amby Fogarty had a lot to answer for when it came to the Dav. "It was all Amby's fault and but for Amby we'd never have heard of Carl Davenport. Amby confided in me as his captain and he said to me one day and we travelling down from a game up the country, he came in and sat down beside me on the bus and he said: 'I have a fellow and I think I can get him over to Cork okay. I said Jesus ... I hope so, we could do with someone and that lad was the Dav." When Amby brought him over everything sort of picked up fairly fast and that was all down to the Dav. The game picked up, the crowds were bigger and our results improved. He was a very good pro and he trained well and he trained hard.

He was great fun and he fitted in well but Amby had singled him out as a figure-head for the team and he wanted to give him a leading role, as it were," explained Noel as Cork Hibs became the dominant force in domestic football. The Dav had a big reputation inside and outside of football but his skipper managed to put a lid on it.

"He wasn't always flamboyant to be fair. He was a genuine character on the football pitch. The dressing room was always funny and full of good banter like all dressing rooms, I suppose, but it was a better place with the Dav around. The Dav brought the craic, the jokes and the banter into ours. I suppose in his few years he helped to lift the whole image of the club and his goals, my word, he scored some magnificent goals not just down the 'Lodge but in every ground in the country," recalled an admiring O'Mahony. "Carl was always about sticking the ball in the bloody net and he got a great thrill and an adrenaline rush from it. His awareness and his alertness in the box was second to none and, even though I

197

keep repeating this, there's no doubt about it but that he was a very good professional and that's probably the best thing that I could say about him," said O'Mahony who, like the rest of his team-mates, was happy to pocket the win bonus on the back of Davenport's goals.

"Look there's a lot of people out there to this day who probably felt the Dav had no real interest in training and couldn't give a feck about it .... but he was always there on time and always did his stint and more."

On the Dav's social engagements and he certainly had a few of them on Leeside, O'Mahony understood as well. "The Dav took a drink okay but I never saw him smoking at all. He was a good boy to have a drink, like the rest of us, but his best pal Wiggie would smoke the lights out. He was always on to Dave (Wigginton) to quit the ciggies. He'd be on to Dave saying: 'Wiggie give up them fecking fags, you fecking eejit, they are bad for you. But sure poor old Wiggie never gave them up. What I remember most about the Dav were his goals, his professionalism and his interest in the club. He had everything and, on top of that, the directors were mad about him as well. It was all down to the fact that, by and large, he was a decent lad anyway and he came from good stock back in England. You can have a fellow come into a club and he's all flash Harry, flamboyant and a bit of a Jack the lad but then he might not be able to back it up where it matters on the park. But Carl could do it. He could back it up and more and he could do it on the pitch where he was judged by the fans over the 90 minutes, if you know what I mean," said Noel who actually played League of Ireland football until he was 41 years of age !

"It was great to have the Dav with us in those days because he was a very genuine guy contrary to what many people might have believed and thought at the time.

It was a masterstroke by Amby (Fogarty) to bring him in around 1967/68 or so.

I think that forward line we had of Tommy Henderson, Carl Davenport, Dave Wigginton and Terry Young out wide was exceptional. They were the best front players that I ever played with or ever saw in the league. They were outstanding and the chief amongst them was the Dav. He loved scoring goals and he had a great will and a desire to win. He got a lot of spectacular goals as well and, I suppose, he built his reputation on that. The Dav got us a fair few wins bonuses in his day but we weren't slow in spending them either," said Noel throwing his head back with laughter.

Some of the standout memories for Noel O'Mahony and the other Hibs players were the annual end-of-season trips to Spain. "We used to go on holiday to Spain at the end of the season and I remember going on, at least, three trips there with the Dav and people like Damien Richardson when he was at Rovers and he'd guest for us.

Ray Cowhie, Austin Noonan, Martin Sheehan and John Brohan and all that gang were on those trips. We'd go on holidays for a week or 10 days after the season ended and it was always the hot-spots in Spain. We played the likes of Espanol and Valencia and so on in a friendly or two (we were lucky they only beat us four-nil) but the Dav, as you can imagine, was head and tail of those trips," said Noel.

"The Dav was a new breed of footballer that Amby Fogarty unearthed and introduced to Ireland but the whole thing took off and it turned out to be a very good spell for Cork

Hibernians and for football in Cork. The Dav was the 'head honcho' as they'd say here in Cork. He used to love ball-hopping Tommy Henderson. Tommy was low-sized you know, and he loved telling stories about him   He loved slating and slagging poor Tommy and Tommy some times couldn't take it and it nearly came to blows once or twice. It was easier for the Dav to pick on him rather than say me or Fada (Martin Sheehan)! He'd have a laugh off all of us to be fair but he was good craic and, I suppose, he made happy days even happier," said Noel by way of tribute to the one and only Carl Davenport.

Carl with his good pals, Mick, Mossie (Roy Keane's Dad)
Tony O'Keeffe and Eddie O'Driscoll

Caption winner: 'How the f**k did I miss that one!' or 'Where did it all go wrong,' The Dav in a solitary, reflective moment at Rochestown Park Hotel in Cork.

Carl with Irish Athletics Champion, Derval O'Rourke at the Mardyke Sports Arena in Cork just days before she went to the Bejing Olympics.
Carl is great friends with her parents Terry and Eva.

JOHN LAWSON & THE "REISLING FEVER"

"Carl Davenport was a unique character when he played here in Cork and I reckon he was the nearest thing we had to George Best in the domestic league.

I think the Dav was probably the worst fellow we had in the club for training along with myself and possibly Carl Humphries. I think we were the worst trainers going in those days and the Dav was top of that list for me. I don't think the Dav and the manager at the time Dave Bacuzzi had any great affinity with one another but, then again, it was Amby Fogarty who brought the Dav to Cork in the first place," said Cork Hibs' dead ball specialist John Lawson when asked to contribute to this football book.

"I don't think Dave really gave 'the Dav' the chances in the first team that he probably deserved. I think maybe if he had played more games for Cork Hibs then he would certainly have proved what a great goal-scorer everyone said he was.

All in all he was a great signing for the two Cork clubs - first Hibs and then Celtic - and he won league medals with both," said John who was one of the stars of that famous Cork Hibs team. The Glasgow-born midfielder played with fellow Scot Sonny Sweeney, now living in Leeds, and Jerry Finnegan in a 4-3-3 set up that Bacuzzi brought to Cork from his days with Manchester City at Maine Road.

The Dav was a good character, good fun and a great lad to be with on a night out with the boys.

We had some good nights in Spain when we used to go on holiday there at the end of the season. The Dav used to like going to the Carousel Club in Hanover Street and we'd always know when he'd been there. He'd come into the dressing room to us after a night on the tiles and he'd be sweating - the drink and the wine - would be coming out his pores and he'd say that he had a touch of 'Reisling fever' today.

He'd be absolutely saturated and the head would be down between his old, bony knees and we'd be asking him: "Hey Dav, you all right or what." "He'd lift his head and say: "Ah don't worry about me - it's just the Riesling fever coming out of me and he'd go and try and run it out of himself   That was one of his famous sayings: "The Carousel ...Who Can Tell ?"

Carl Davenport was a big name in Cork, driving around in his Sunbeam Rapier and when he arrived and built a name for himself in the League of Ireland, he added five or six thousand to the gates down the 'Lodge and at Turner's Cross where he later became player-manager at Cork Celtic. The fans used to come in their droves down to Flower Lodge especially to see him play at his peak. Lawson recalled: "We had a few other big names in that Hibs team but I think the fact that he scored all those goals helped to make him as a player and certainly helped built up his reputation in the game." "It was funny because one day the Dav missed a penalty down the 'Lodge and that was probably the start of my reign as penalty taker within the club. I was totally and utterly left-footed, the right was purely for standing on, and I think that helped me with the dead ball situations and I just had this happy knack of being able to find the net. The Dav had skill to burn but obviously he wasn't blessed with the pace of say Terry Young, Miah Dennehy or say Dave Wigginton.

He made up for it with the bit of skill he had, the close control and being in the right place at the right time when the ball came into the box.

He could read the game well and he was a great character to have in the side.

There was never a dull moment with the Dav, on or off the park, and he could make things happen. He played best

203

between the midfielders and the forwards and he was very good at linking the play - that was his forte rather than playing balls in behind defenders," said Lawson of those heady days on Leeside. "He was good to have around because he could break the ice in a tense situation in the dressing room and I even remember after losing the league to Waterford that day down the 'Lodge, the Dav was the one that lifted the team's spirits and tried to lift the gloom. He brought a light-heartedness and a sense of humour to it and I think he had a role to play in getting us all back up for the Cup final the following Sunday when we went to Dalymount Park to play the same Waterford team - the new league champions - and we trashed them with Miah's (Dennehy's) historic hat-trick."

"I remember we had a players' meeting after the League decider on the Tuesday and we ironed out a few things. A lot of us were not too pleased with what had been said and written about us after the league decider but I think we got over it quick enough.

We lifted ourselves and we got the job done the following Sunday with the cup win but it still rankles that we let a double slip through our hands," said Lawson who now lives on Magazine Road on the south side of the city. The Dav's escapades around town are legendary and John takes up the mantle. "The Dav was well-known around town and he was a good man to socialise in those days. He'd come into training in the evening - all the boys would be arriving in their working gear from Fords and Dunlops and wherever and ready for the night shift. The Dav would breeze in with his 'going-out' clothes on a hanger - his suit, shirt and tie and his little bag with his brush and comb - the whole lot - and ready for the off. You might not see the Dav until two or three in the morning after that - if you saw him at all! He was out and about a fair bit and he knew how to enjoy himself. I think we all picked up a few tips from him in that regard. He might be out late but he'd be in for training okay the following morning. We used to dread the Tuesday mornings after a game when the gaffer would suggest Beaumont Quarry for a session and I know Carl was often tempted to duck away, make an excuse or whatever to get out of the dreaded quarry sessions. It was hell, believe me ... we used to carry one another up the steep incline in the quarry and we'd be up and down the steps of the main stand as well. It was mainly runs, sprints and jogging from the corner flag or the goalposts to the half-way line and back and, to be honest, we actually didn't do a lot of ball work. It was all about stamina, strength and match fitness with Bacuzzi and, in those days, there wasn't a great deal of ball work but then we only had five or six of us as full-time pros. I used to stay back on occasion to practice my free kicks." The money and wages in the game in Ireland in recent years has spiraled out of control and landed so many clubs in financial troubles but back in the early 70's the wages from football were in and around a tenner a week, at best. "We were on a quid a point .. that was the bonus we were on but the Dav was on good money at Hibs and probably even more when he was player-manager at Cork Celtic.

My own wages at the time varied between £22 and £25 quid a week as a full-timer so it wasn't too bad. What stands out for me whenever I think of the Dav were the two goals he scored for us in the Blaxnit Cup final down the 'Lodge against Coleraine.

They were two exceptional goals, two fabulous goals, one after the other. He amazed us all that afternoon with the quality of those two strikes and I think the penny dropped then for a lot of the lads and we knew he had talent.

The other abiding memory I have of him was when he introduced me to the late Alan Ball who had won a World Cup winners medal with England in 1966 at Wembley.

That was a day I will never forget. The Dav was marvellous friends with 'Bally' and we all met up in Cork. I don't have a bad word to say about the Dav and I am sure he'd be the same about me. He was generally a right-footed player but he wasn't great in the air 'cause that would ruin his hairstyle. He wasn't the biggest of men but he was brave and he wouldn't shirk anything on the football field.

It's true what they say ..... he was a one off," said the Scottish-born Lawson who was the heartbeat of that famous Cork Hibs team of the late 1960's and early 70's.

FRANK CONNOLLY

Frank Connolly, good pals with Christy Ring and the Kerry legend that is Mick O'Connell, rarely if ever paid for his breakfast on the train to Dublin for away games.

The lads up in the dining car in the old days on the way to play Shamrock Rovers, Shelbourne or St. Pat's used to toss to see who would end up footing the bill and, according to Frank, invariably, it was the gaffer Dave Bacuzzi who would be 'stung' with the bill.

Frankie Connolly from Blackrock was a valued member of Cork Hibernians squad in the 70's and a good pal of Carl Davenport's as well. He played his schoolboy soccer with Ringmahon Rangers and was capped for Ireland U15s against England and Wales in 1960 playing on the left-wing and his inside partner was Eamon Dunphy !

Frankie made his debut for Cork Hibs in the 1966-67 Shield competition playing as an attacking inside left and scored five goals in his debut season.

206

Towards end of his second season, he was converted to the full-back role and wore the No 2 shirt with distinction. When new player manager Dave Bacuzzi arrived in 1970/71 Frankie moved across to the other flank and was ever present in the left-full position. He also became an accomplished central defender and went on to win League Championship, two FAI Cups, Shield and Blaxnit Trophy medals with Hibs.

"I remember we were playing Linfield in the Blaxnit Cup up at Windsor Park at the height of the troubles and they beat us 1-0 the same night. But we were having a jar afterwards in the Linfield clubhouse and we came out to get on the Ulster Bus to get us back as far as the border. I was sitting across from the Dav and Wiggie was inside me in the window seat. The bus was just warming up, purring away for the trip south and just as we pulled off a brick came through the window on the other side.

It shattered the glass but then a second brick came right through the window and you'd want to see the Dav diving for cover. He's down on his knees in the centre isle shouting out: "Christ, there's a busload of Paddy's here and two of their own. Who did they throw the fecking brick at ? Do they realise there's two good Protestants on the bus." "I said to him off you go so and tell them to lay off.

The second time the window and the glass came in on top of us and I looked down at him and said: 'There you are now, paying for your sins. I said you were running the channels again tonight but I knew I'd see you one day on your knees."

The Dav was always running the channels when he was in Cork but we never quite knew was it the north channel or the south channel !

The Dav was a great character to have around the club and with his ready wit, good sense of humour and charm, he slotted in well with the Hibs camp in those days.

"Listen he was the life and soul of the party and we had a fair few parties in those days. I was down in Kinsale one day when I was working for Coca-Cola. I was finished the delivery and I was on my way home and just outside the supermarket I saw this pair of feet on the ground. I said to the helper - 'Jesus I know them feet' and the young lad thought I was going off my chuck like. I stopped the truck anyway and I got out and walked over and there he was stretched out on the footpath between the cars. It was a handsome day and there he was, the Dav, sun-bathing away.

He looks up at me and says: "How did you know I was here ? I said to him well I saw your feet and you must have the only tanned pair of feet in Kinsale.

We'd just come back, you see, from one of those end-of-season trips to Spain and the Dav had been out all f...ing night and had the two feet up to the sun during the day. You couldn't miss him! The Dav was fond of Kinsale, his little haven by the sea and to this day he still goes back to visit friends there. "There was another day in Kinsale when he had no petrol in the Jag and I had to give him a few bob to get a can of petrol up at Dempsey's garage to get himself back to Cork. The first thing he did when he came into training on the Saturday morning was to walk straight up to me and give me the few bob back. Fair play to him, he was that type of guy and he was fierce honest. Outside of being a great character, he was honest as the day is long and we all admired that about him. I would trust him with my life anyway," says Connolly who keeps in touch with Carl and occasionally they have a jar together up at Frankie's local - the Kerryman's in Dillon's Cross.

The Dav has a great affinity with Cork city and he loves the place. He just keeps coming back year after year. It's over 35 years ago since he was a player here with Cork Hibs and Cork Celtic but he continues to come back almost every year without fail.   It's amazing too the number of people who remember him from all those years ago and come up and have a chat with him.   He's a charismatic figure with so many football fans ... it's unbelievable and Connolly can vouch for that too.

"He was a fabulous player and he was deadly in and around the penalty area. He lived for the goals he scored and he always seemed to be in the right place at the right time.

He was a good team player, a good worker and he never played for himself. He only played for the team. He was an excellent player and while John Lawson had a terrific left foot, the Dav had a great right peg and they could both score goals from set pieces.

The Dav had great power in his shots and I have seen him score some wonderful goals. I suppose, we had the best of both worlds at Hibs with the Dav and 'Lawso' in our team," said Frank as he recalled some of the Dav's footballing feats.

"He turned out to be a very good friend of mine and no matter where you'd run into him, he'd make a point of coming up and chatting to you.

A lot of the friendships he made in football in the 1960's and 70's when he played in Cork, are as solid today as they were over 30 years ago and it's nice to be able to say that about him. He brought something special to Cork soccer and he added thousands to the gates wherever he played.   I remember playing down the 'Lodge in front of no more than 400 or 500 people but once the Dav and Amby Fogarty arrived on the scene everything changed for the better. The crowds shot up and we had an influx of players like Dave Wigginton, Tony Marsden, Barry Notley, Richie Brooks, Tommy Henderson and Freddy Ellison and they were great characters."

Connolly added: "The Dav came to Cork Celtic first and then to Hibs but he was only 23 when he was player-manager at Celtic - the youngest ever in the League of Ireland.

I was surprised when he left Hibs and went back to Celtic for a second spell but then Dave Bacuzzi had arrived at the 'Lodge and I don't think they really saw eye to eye like.

Tony Marsden arrived too and the Dav was player-manager at Turner's Cross.

But that made no difference to him in the least and he was still your buddy.

He actually had three stints at Cork Celtic, won league medals at Hibs and with Celtic in 1974 and also had a spells in junior football with Killeagh in east Cork and with Crosshaven before hanging up his famous boots."

The Dav still wears that first league winners' medal he got with Cork Hibs around his neck and has done so since the very day he won it in the mid-70's .... that's what it all meant to him.

RAY COWHIE

"I was captain of Cork Celtic in 1967 and Donie Leahy was vice-captain and the directors invited us to go to the Metropole Hotel to meet a new player and there we met the Dav who arrived in his Sunbeam Rapier. We ended up going for a drink in a very famous pub at the time in Cork - McAuliffe's bar in Merchant Street.

It's now well gone like Roches Stores but it was over there at the back of the old Roches Stores. It was a grand quiet pub with a snug in the corner where we met the Dav, with Donie and I all ending up in there. At closing time, the Dav says is there any nightclubs around. I can't remember if it was a Friday or a Saturday night but we had a game on the Sunday.

Anyway we pointed him in the direction of the Arcadia and left him to it. He was out the following day anyway and he scored two fine goals having been down the Arc and that was my first meeting with the Dav.

He was a real man about town in those days but he could do the business on the pitch and he was a big hit with the Cork Celtic fans. He became player-manager of Cork Celtic then and he brought over Alan Ball's father- Alan senior - to show us some modern training techniques and skills and so on. He signed Tony "Tucker" Allen, John McCarthy and Pat O'Mahony and I remember we had a fairly good side.

The Dav scored a lot of goals that season but apart from being manager, he was the groundsman as well and I can see him now cutting the grass out the 'Cross.

He was totally immersed in the club and totally caught up in it and for the away matches he used to put the car - a green Zephyr Zodiac - at the disposal of the club and he'd drive us to the away fixtures.

It would be me, Tucker Allen, Donie (Leahy) and the Dav would do the driving himself. That was our car load on match days.

"I remember one day we were on the way to Sligo and we stopped off at Athlone and we had something to eat but we'd lost the car carrying the directors - they took a wrong turn. We got to Sligo on the Saturday night and checked in and the Dav says will we go out for a drink. We had a few pints before the directors came and there was a sing-song started. The local Sligo lads in the bar asked the Dav were we a showband and he says: "No, we are Cork Celtic and we are playing Sligo Rovers tomorrow." We beat Sligo 5-1 the next day.

"It was in 1969 when Amby Fogarty signed the Dav and I was signed for Cork Hibs as well. The Dav was out in Grange and he had two young kids at the time.

He rang me one morning to pick him up for training because his car was broken down. I collected him anyway and when I went into the house, the place was freezing. We got into the car and he told me he has the heating okay but he couldn't afford it. The next night, I picked him up again to go training and called to the house again. This time it was like a Turkish bath inside with the heat and so on and I guessed he'd got some money from somewhere to pay the bill.

But naw .... he showed me where he had put some cellotape around the wheel of the meter to stop it moving and that was the Dav at his best!

"I remember on another occasion we went to Spain with Hibs to play a few games in the summer. We got the train to Dublin and there was these two girls on the train.

They were reps for an Australian canned fruit company. They were two fine looking women and anyway the Dav, of course, was chatting them up on the train.

We arrived at the Castle Hotel at the top of O'Connell Street but there was no sign of the Dav. The following morning, we were on O'Connell Street waiting to get the bus to the airport and he shows up just in time. He told me he'd stayed in the Gresham with the two girls.

We got out to Spain anyway and we played Loret-de-Mar, a third division side and we beat them 4-0. But two days later, the word came down that the Dav had taken ill and we'd have to get a doctor to have a look at him. All we were told by the directors was that he was confined to bed and he'd a fierce temperature. It transpired that he'd got a 'dose' off one of the Aussie girls!

The Dav was a very good player to be fair to him and he was a great passer of the ball and a great lad to get goals. He was always in the right spot to turn the ball into the net. He was good in the air too and while he wasn't blessed with great pace, he worked hard for the team. He got himself up and down the pitch and he wouldn't just hang around and wait for things to happen. He actually made things happen to be fair. He was a good link player and kept moves and attacks going and he played his best football between the midfield men and the forwards. He used to get a lot of goals coming from deep but he was well built and a tough character.

Ray and the Dav ended their playing careers together when they had a season at junior side Killeagh on the road to Youghal in east Cork. "The Dav was signed up as player-manager of Killeagh and he asked me to come along so we had one season there and it was a just a howl there. It was a scream and we really enjoyed it before we bowed out. We had a good laugh and they looked after us well. We used to use the Thatch Inn there on the bridge - one of the oldest pubs in Ireland - as a base. The man who owned it was on the committee so after training we'd go to the Thatch for a pint and we'd have a steak and chips free gratis as well.

I only played junior one season with Killeagh but it turned out to be one of the most enjoyable and I am sure the Dav would say the exact same."

CORK CITY SPORTS

Very recently I was invited up to Collins Barracks, as I have said before I love the place, and the people, it was a launch for the Cork City Sports, which were being held at the new Stadium up at the Mardyke.

Myself and my pal the late Frank O'Brien of 96FM, and my great friend from the Irish Examiner Michael Ellard, arrive there at 2pm and enter a lovely big room in the officers quarter. It's a full house with food and drink provided, the Lord Mayor, photographers and a mixture of people involved in the Cork City Sports.

It's a big event as some of the athletes who will be competing for places to perform in Beijing, at the Olympic Games are present.

Gone are my days, when I was the Lancashire champion at 400yds, and also the high jump, now I could not run and jump on a moving bus, how sad is that, but I can still jump in bed? That's dedication for you!

Getting back to the reception, I see a friend of mine Terry O'Rourke, who used to live near me in Donnybrook, Douglas, with his wife Eva, this is 30 years ago, and they had no children, I say "What you doing here?", Oh I like athletics, half an hour later she says I am going to Beijing, "very nice" I say, Oh! I am the Secretary of the City Sports, another ten minutes later. After being fed all this information over the best part of an hour, and a few drinks, a couple of photographs he finally tells me (typical Cork man) that his daughter, whom I didn't know he had, her name was Derval and she was running in the Beijing Olympic Games, and won a gold medal in the 60m hurdles at the World indoor championships in Moscow and a silver in the 100m hurdles in the European Championships in Gothenburg. So thanks Terry for finally telling me that you really did not put me back in the kennel.

So Saturday arrives and off I go to the City Sports with my friend who was over from England, Paul Clement and what a great day we had, we had V.I.P. passes and were taken up to the press room, were Frank was commentating for 96FM. We had a coffee and a bite to eat, and who is sitting in there on her own only the lovely Derval, I ask how's her Dad and that I used to live near him years ago and I had met him a few days before at the launch. She says I know who you are, I thought she was going to say that old fucker, who played a bit of soccer but she was too polite. She ran a great race later and her come back looks like it's on track, a dedicated athlete and a lovely person which is always good to see, and that comes from good parents, well done! Well I wish her the best for the forthcoming games and in her life to come, and when I am proud to have had my photograph taken with her that says a lot coming from me, as there are not many who reach that platform in life and from me that is a compliment

Well the sports are nearly over now so myself and Paul head down the Mardyke to No.1 Maryville, opposite the Cricket Ground, which was the first place I lived when I arrived in Cork January 1967, (was you born/ then the house was owned as I said earlier by Mr & Mrs Dan Hartnett, what great times they were, so as you can see from the photo, I did have to have one taken, as it sent me spinning back to those fantastic days and nights in that golden era. My room was the attic at the top of the house with a great view of the doctor's daughters who lived opposite on Western Road. When I think back to that time 23 years old I had the lot, new car, great digs, player manager of Cork Celtic and as many women as I could handle.

I thought all my birthdays had come together, its only now I realise how lucky I was and the circumstances in England that guided me to this beautiful place called Cork, and I will always be grateful.

Carl with Noel Spillane and Kerry legend Mick O'Connell on Valentia Island

A DAY WITH MICK O'CONNELL

EARLY in the year, I made arrangements to go down to Valentia Island, off the coast of Kerry with my soccer pal Noel Spillane.

The purpose of the trip was to meet up with Kerry Gaelic football legend Mick O'Connell, who is now in his early seventies.

Myself and Noel set off early one winter morning and on our two hour journey from Cork we chatted as we drove along, and a few stories thrown in, we stopped for lunch in a very famous place called Killorglin.

For hundreds of years they have a fair here called "Puck Fair" in which they celebrate and crown a goat and people come from all over the world to enjoy the festival and the craic.

It's a very big occasion with sideshows, bands and Irish dancers and the drink flows for the few days of the festival.

After a nice lunch in the Bianconi bar we were back on the road and on our way to Valentia and what superb scenery we passed along the way.

The lakes and mountains and green fields and hedgerows were jaw dropping beauty for a lad like me from the back streets of Farnworth near Bolton.

And nearing our destination I caught a glimpse of the vast Atlantic Ocean and it took my breath away.

A few miles back the road we passed Kate Kearney's Cottage and the Gap of Dungloe and again the scenery was magnificent .. no wonder they call the county of Kerry the Kingdom.

The ferry on the Portmagee side is not running - closed in winter - so we have to go over the causeway and on to the island itself.

We drive the length of the island through Castletown and right down to the harbour and the lifeboat station at Knightstown.

I suppose it's the capital of Valentia Island - a few pubs, a shop, a cafe and a church but we hadn't seen a human being as yet !

We get out of the car and stretch our legs with a short walk along the sea front.

Back we get in the car and Mick had told me to just ask anyone where he lived and they would give us directions to his house.

We drove back up the main street to the fork in the road by the church and there is old gentleman learning over the wall.

I put the passenger window down and ask: " Do you know where Mick O'Connell lives ?"

Well as all Kerrymen do he answered my enquiry with a question or two of his own.

Firstly he wanted to know where we were from but he had a good idea with the "C" registration on the car and then he wanted to know had I played football with Micko.

Answer to the first question - "Yes, down from Cork" and I said yes to the second. Both were little white lies, I suppose.

So we follow the man's directions but typically two city lads down on a day trip we get lost and go way past Micko's abode.

We turn the car around and head back down the hill and ask again for directions to be told that there is Mick's car heading off down the road about 500 yards in front of us.

It wasn't long before Mick was coming back up the road against us – flashing his lights - so our friend outside the old churchyard had given him the low down on us.

We finally get to our destination and get to meet the great man.

We are standing and chatting outside his lovely home overlooking the sea and all of a sudden Mick disappears into an outhouse.

Lo and behold … out he emerges with an O'Neill's football and we start taking penalties into the garage door.

I can tell you now he is still a very fit man and has lost none of his passion and skill with the ball at his feet.

He is well read and well up on English and Spanish soccer and knows more about La Liga and the Bundesliga than I do !

Inside the house and sitting in a bay window overlooking the sea, his wife Rosaleen makes us afternoon tea.

Micko shows us around the house and shows us some of the interesting things he's collected over the years and he shows us a map of the pipe laying route of the Morse Code to America.

I'd drive the 200 or so miles all the way to Valentia any day of the week just to have a chat with the great Mick O'Connell.

It was a wonderful experience for me to get to meet him and he's one of the nicest people I have ever met.

It was a day trip that will stay with me for the rest of my life and today's sports men and women could take a leaf out of Micko's book .. humble, sincere and a man with a great passion for sport.

Mick I know you watched me playing soccer down the 'Lodge and out the 'Cross and I watched you in the Kerry jersey at Croke Park and elsewhere all those years ago but thanks for the memories and for a great day on beautiful Valentia Island. I will treasure it for the rest of my life.

Extract from Evening Echo, December, 2009

AT LAST the Dav's book is out and here Echo soccer writer, NOEL SPILLANE talks to Kerry legend Mick O'Connell who features prominently in the publication.

AS actor Michael Caine was prone to say: 'Not too many people know that' and such a statement certainly holds true in the context of Carl's autobiography.

You see Kerry legend Mick O'Connell was a big sporting hero of Carl's in the 1960's but what many did not realise was that 'the Dav' was just as big a sporting icon for the famous Valentia Islander who still lives in full view of the lighthouse at the entrance to Knightstown harbour.

And such a fan of the Dav's and Hibs and Celtic, was Micko in those days that he ignored the GAA ban at the time to go and see the Dav in action down the 'Lodge.

"I gave a year of my life to Cork and to UCC in the old days and they used to get great crowds at the soccer down the 'Lodge, the Mardyke and at Turner's Cross.

Afterwards when Cork Hibs played at Flower Lodge and they were going well with Carl in the team, I used to go and see them play.

I visited the 'Lodge a few times okay to see him play and I was delighted to go up there.

It was great that Cork soccer was strong enough in those days to bring a few Englishmen over to play here and Carl Davenport was one of the first.

The introduction of players like Dave Wigginton, Tony Marsden, Keith Edwards and Carl gave a real lift to the domestic game," explained Mick when the Dav and I met him over Christmas on Valentia Island.

"I thought that was a great initiative on behalf of Cork Hibs

220

and I think Cork Celtic followed their example afterwards.

I have great memories of those days and going to Flower Lodge with over 20,000 in the grounds.

I had seven or eight months in UCC at the time but then I got a job back home here in Valentia, and in those days that was the way it was, if you got a job, you took it," said Micko as we enjoyed tea and biscuits and that splendid view from his home overlooking the lighthouse.

The thing about Mick O'Connell in those heady days was that a lot of people saw him as a bit of a recluse but that was not the Mick O'Connell who enthralled us in December with his knowledge and expertise of English and Spanish football and his interest in Ireland's World Cup bid.

"It was great to see these 'foreign' players coming in to play here in Cork and around the League of Ireland and as Carl said he got good wages and so on.

But it gave another flavour to the game in Cork in the 1960's and 70's and it's something that is, unfortunately, missing in the game today.

I would like to see all sports thriving and I still follow the majority of them.

Carl certainly made an impact and I was there to see it.

He is still remembered with great fondness to this day by many of us who saw him play at his peak," recalled O'Connell.

"The ban was in but it was weakening at the time. Personally, I felt the ban was a bit too ridiculous because sport should be independent of politics. They just don't mix.

I didn't care about personalities - it was the actual playing of the game that I admired.

I would like to see sport for what it is .... fair play and something way beyond any personal differences.

I saw soccer played in England too and I saw sportsmanship

there - play and let play - but in the modern game when I see a corner coming across and players pulling and dragging one another and the acceptance of that type of fouling, it really saddens me.

I think that type of thing has degraded soccer and it would not have been tolerated in the old days," said Mick who won four All-Irelands, 12 provincial titles and an All-Star with the Kingdom between 1956 and 1973.

And the Kerry GAA legend is well up on all sports and enjoys watching Barcelona and Real Madrid on Sky, keeps right up to speed with Declan Kidney's Ireland rugby team in the Six Nations as well.

"I suppose I am well up on sport but I watch a lot of soccer and rugby on the telly and I can get that here in Valentia now thanks to Sky Sports.

Sometimes it clashes with other events that my wife might want see, but as far as possible, I get to watch all the big games and I do enjoy it.

I feel privileged that I can be living here on Valentia, miles from anywhere and on a bad evening, weather-wise, or any other evening, I can watch top class sport in the comfort of my own home. That is great and that is technology at its best," Micko told me.

"But I suppose the downside of it is that not too many young people now are playing the game - they are watching it instead. Its great to watch it but I'd prefer to see them out practicing the skills of their chosen sport in their own time. I suppose it's the way life is gone now."

Mick has a fondness for Arsenal but that comes through his handicapped son Diarmuid who is a big Gunners fan.

"I don't necessarily have a favourite team but my young lad, Diarmuid has been over to see the Arsenal a few times.

And, I suppose, to satisfy him I like to see them do well. They play a lovely brand of football but they are not as successful as some of the other teams.

I admire the way they play the game and in the broader appeal of the game, you have to admire the skills of players like Lionel Messi .... and I do," he told me.

O'Connell still goes to see Kerry play at Croke Park on All-Ireland final day and sets off from Valentia at the crack of dawn on All-Ireland Sunday to get the train from Tralee to the capital.

"I go up to the All-Irelands at Croke Park still but the biggest thrill I got out of Gaelic football was to be able to field the ball well and bring my team-mates into play.

It wasn't all about the winning or losing of matches but to be part of a great Kerry team.

I loved challenging myself on the football field and fielding was a key element of the game when I played it.

To be honest, it's very much a hand ball game now and it's semi-basketball on grass.

Kicking off the ground is a skill that's almost gone and not valued.

I think a game without skills is not worth much. I don't say that now to denigrate the players - it's not the players I am talking about - it's the skill factor, the actual play. The rules of Gaelic football were always questionable and, to me, they are chopping and changing far too much," said O'Connell as he challenged the GAA and Croke Park to have a fresh look at the rule book.

"They have no idea as to how to frame a set of rules to give to young boys and say this is the game and this is what you can and cannot do. Any game that is not clearly defined is a bit of a tuppenny-halfpenny game to me," said Micko.

What about the All-Ireland Mick?

"Well I don't get parochial about it - I don't really care. Look if it were Fermanagh and Louth playing in the final or Cork and Donegal, I'd go to it hoping to be entertained.

I don't get too carried away on the Kerry bias or anything like that - good play is what I like to see on All-Ireland final day - and so be it if I get it.

I don't go to that many games to be honest because the game is not something that I admire - the type of play is not what it should be.

I am not getting at the players because they put a lot of time, effort and energy into it but it's the actual play that gets to me. It's evolved into a very basketball-type of game now and there's too much negativity in it," says Micko of the modern game where pulling and dragging is the norm.

He says it takes from the game as a spectacle and he's right.

As Micko warms to the topic of conversation and pours another cup of tea for us he recalls another famous story of his day.

"We had a man here Paddy Dennehy who worked in the Irish Army and he was trained by a Swedish masseur in the art of massage.

I would train hard and practice a lot on my own here in Valentia but before matches if I could get across to him he would give me a proper massage and get me right.

I saw the benefit of that and I was often recommending him to the Kerry County Board but they won't tolerate it or accept it at the time.

Sure at the time, we'd go to a game and we'd have no ball for the warm-up.

They reckoned at the time that it would be a bit ostentatious of us.

I used to say to them - how can you be warming up or be fit to play well unless you had the 'feel' of the ball and to get your eye in.

It was the ethos of the time and, I suppose, who was I a lone man here from an island but they have listened to people since," he quipped as we watched the waves breaking over the rocks under the lighthouse.

The Dav says: "Meeting the great Mick O'Connell after all these years and down at his home place on Valentia Island is a day I will never, ever forget, I will take it with me to the grave."

Carl with Kerry GAA legend Mick O'Connell at Mick's home on Valentia Island

Carl's TV interview best I've seen yet

Deputy Lord Mayor John Murray, Carl Davenport, Rita Hansford and Austin Noonan at City Hall.

Dav is always an entertainer

IT'S the characters that give sport its colour and Irish soccer has always had plenty of them.

One of the greats was Carl Davenport, the Englishman who graced some of the most brilliant Cork Celtic and Cork Hibernians teams during a glorious era.

It was great to see Carl was back on Leeside lately and Neil Prendeville did an excellent interview with him on Multichannel during the week.

It was an entertaining chat, because Carl was always a superb entertainer, both on and off the field.

Sussed

Today's young people may think they've got it sussed but the night spots of Cork were pretty hot back in the 60s too and Carl Davenport, as a young star soccer player was well placed to enjoy them.

He gave us a flavour of that time in his interview and it was nice to see that he still seems to be enjoying life to the full.

IT was real nostalgia to see Neil Prendeville's interview on Multichannel television during the week with the legendary Carl Davenport.

It certainly was the best TV I have seen in years.

In my opinion Davenport was the best soccer player ever to grace a League of Ireland pitch.

His personality was on par with his gifted talent as a footballer, which made him a very well respected and admired sports star not only in Cork but nation-wide.

The Flower Lodge days are now very much in the past, but the interview with Mr Nice Guy Carl Davenport was, to say the least, a much welcomed 'flashback' to the late '60s and early '70s when Cork soccer was to many almost a religion.

Eugene Cosgrove
Mallow
Co. Cork

● *Have you any memories of the great days of Flower Lodge, Turner's Cross or the Markets Field? Why not put pen to paper and let us know?*

Billy Morgan signs for Cork Celtic

CORK AND MUNSTER senior football goalkeeper, Billy Morgan, has signed for League of Ireland club, Cork Celtic, writes Michael Ellard.

Rated the most outstanding goalkeeper in Gaelic football at present, Morgan was signed by Celtic player-manager, Carl Davenport on Friday last when regular goalkeeper Alec Ludzic went down with 'flu. Morgan, however, was unable to travel to Ballybofey with the Celtic team because of an intermediate hurling league final with his club, Nemo Rangers.

Some newspaper clippings feraturing the Dav

226